A POCKET HISTORY OF SEX

in the

TWENTIETH CENTURY

A POCKET HISTORY OF SEX

in the

TWENTIETH CENTURY

[*a memoir*]

Jane Vandenburgh

COUNTERPOINT

BERKELEY

The author is grateful for the encouragement of the editors of the following
publications, in which some of this book's materials appeared in earlier forms:
Nimrod, the *Los Angeles Times Magazine*, *Image Magazine*,
and San Francisco's *Focus Magazine*.

The author's understanding of the physical ordeal undertaken by those who
walked two thousand miles from Independence, Missouri, to settle the West
is indebted to Keith Heyer Meldahl's magnificent *Hard Road West:
History and Geology Along the Gold Rush Trail*.

Library of Congress Cataloging-in-Publication Data

VANDENBURGH, JANE.
A pocket history of sex in the twentieth century : a memoir / Jane Vandenburgh.
p. cm.
ISBN 978-1-58243-459-9
1. Vandenburgh, Jane. I. Title.

PS3572.A65 Z46
813'.54—dc22

2008035702

Paperback ISBN: 978-1-58243-559-6

Cover design by Natalya Balnova
Interior design by Megan Cooney
Printed in the United States of America

COUNTERPOINT
2560 Ninth Street
Suite 318
Berkeley, CA 94710

www.counterpointpress.com

THIS IS A WORK of nonfiction whose events happened in the real world. I have, however, employed some of the techniques of fiction in order to tell the story that exists most vividly in my recollections. I have also changed the names of some of the participants in order to protect their identities.

For my aunt, Janet Vandenburgh Godfrey,
who didn't get the starring role in this production, but is nevertheless its hero.

CONTENTS

it seems they were all cheated of some marvellous experience

which is not going to go wasted on me which is why I'm telling you about it

—FRANK O'HARA

A POCKET HISTORY OF SEX

in the

TWENTIETH CENTURY

1

THE PULL OF GRAVITY

1

Normalcy

THE LAST HOUSE I will live in with both my parents and my two brothers is one built on a sandy lot in Redondo, a development in a beach town near Los Angeles. Our house is distinguished only by the pepper tree our father planted out in front, where other, more normal dads would dump topsoil and then scatter lawn seed. The house is new, but there isn't any hope for it. It smells of wet cement, as if something is wrong with its foundation. Cold leaks upward through the floorboards, drawing body heat down and out of our bare feet, back to the lot's damp sand.

My brothers and I are blond, tan, tousle-haired beach rats, seriously unkempt. Will and Geo and I know, because one of our more elegant San Marino relatives told us, that we are being raised "by Gawd." "By Gawd, quite obviously, since John and Maggie cannot be bawwthured." Our parents' parenting is described by our Aunt Nan as *benign neglect.*

My brothers and I know no discipline. We wander for miles, going off to the beach or to the pier to fish. We ride our bikes on the esplanade and come home late, idly poking sticks into the already rotting stucco on the outside of the houses to get at the scraps of tar paper, which we pull out and chew like gum.

It is the 1950s, and both of our parents—who come from privileged backgrounds—believe they've ended up in this dump because their money and their luck ran out. Luck is no longer John and Maggie's specialty. They can still count on one or the other set of grandparents, however, to swoop in to fix things when they mess up. My grandparents say it's always trouble whenever the phone rings and it concerns Maggie and Johnny. That's when they have to make phone calls to The Powers That Be, or help my parents out financially. Buying them this house at the beach in Redondo may be one of their last-ditch attempts, getting a starter home for people no longer starting out.

Redondo is an object lesson: How Normal People Are Content to Live.

Other families seem less ambiguous about what you're supposed to do. You get this job. You buy that house. You raise your children. You build a foursquare life, you go forever to live in it.

On Avenue B in Redondo, our parents are losing any wish they've ever had to fit in. Folks believe in America as a Melting Pot, in which everyone urgently needs to learn to conform. The Melting Pot reminds me of Little Black Sambo, who is chased by a tiger around a tree every Saturday morning on cartoons: They go round and round until they melt together into butter.

Redondo is *I Love Lucy*, which I hate for its noisy domestic chaos, and *My Little Margie*, which I like because Gale Storm has a good haircut and a job she keeps from week to week. The name Gale Storm also contains the one grown-up joke I understand.

There is little about being an adult that is clear to me. What I do know is that the foursquare life doesn't impress my parents. Homeownership does nothing for them, either. Homeownership involves housekeeping, home maintenance, staying in one place. And awwwctually? our mother remarks as she swooshes her paintbrush around in the bright dyes she uses to paint on Bristol board. Truuuthfully? I'd *much* prefer to move.

Homeownership is a family tradition; real estate is what amounts to almost a family religion, everything being predicated on growth, on the ever-skyward direction of California land values. Everyone in our family has always owned houses, plural—the main one in town and also the ratty dream shack in the mountains or up the coast in Cambria, or at the beach for the summertime, when—like all real Californians—you hike and fish and swim. You very vehemently *picnic*, as my mother says, or you *are forced* to camp out in those gawd-awful sleeping bags on the wretched sleeping porch that is never heated, in order to simulate being in the tyrannical Out of Doors.

My god how I hate *na-chur*, our mother likes to say, how it's all red in tooth and claw.

She says these things to any and all who listen as she works at the kitchen table, where she is painting the storyboards she makes for Disney. Homeownership doesn't make you *a good person*, she says. The Vandenburgh Seniors *awwwwnd* the Whites *awwwwnd* the Ainsworth-Rutherford-Rolands all own *houses, plural,* she goes on, and did we imagine this was anything that got them immediately into their version of heaven? Honestly?

She glances up from what she is doing, one eye winked shut against the upward bloom of her cigarette smoke. She then flicks her gaze over the four corners of her work.

Honestly? she asks again. Just look how crappily *they* turned out.

She inhales smoke, changes brushes in the water jar. Shitheels, she pronounces, whispering to herself.

Ours is a blue-collar neighborhood where the kids are tough and the fathers—cops, plumbers, workers in tool-and-die—will beat up a son who seems to be turning out to be a pansy. No one aside from our father—who is an architect—drives off to work on Wilshire Boulevard on the Miracle Mile wearing a dark suit, white dress shirt, and bowtie. No one aside from our artist mother acts like she does, sitting at the kitchen table, drinking beer and smoking cigarettes, as she first inks in and then colors the Donald Duck comics that will be printed over Walt Disney's famous signature. There is no one else playing Bartôk, as our father does late into the evening, on the baby grand that takes up too much of the tiny living room.

There is bingo in our neighborhood and there is bowling, but my parents don't go.

My parents can neither abide the normal world—the house, the marriage, the children—nor exit it entirely. They aren't rich enough to afford their privacy. They won't live long enough to find the more tolerant cultural atmosphere my brothers and I will someday enjoy (and even that tolerance will sometimes seem like a window only, one that is opened to let in light and air, but that can easily be slammed down and shuttered again).

Our little beach house is full of big, heavy, old-fashioned furniture that our parents inherited from Various Dead Rich Relatives Who Never Gave a Damn About Us When They Were Alive, as our mother will explain to anyone even vaguely interested. These dead relatives include enfeebled grammas and great-aunts and uncles who tend to live across the Los Angeles Basin in the leafier, more prosperous suburbs. Our parents don't actually *want* this furniture, which arrives unbidden by truck from Pasadena or Santa Monica, as these are artifacts of the fancy Vandenburghs, the Ainsworth-Rutherford-Rolands, the Moseses, the Whites, all that is *ritzy fitz,* she says, very high up, dontcha know, in all the la-dee-da crap. They were wellborn, while we are Class Damage.

My parents' bedroom furniture, which is huge, mahogany, and ornately carved, came to them from our father's Grandmama Nell. It is so massive that it needed to be taken apart and then rebuilt in their bedroom. There is also a bureau and a dresser and night tables. The solid headboard is so tall it reaches almost to the ceiling, so wide it has to be pushed diagonally back against the bedroom's corner windows.

Oh Jesus Fucking Christ, our mother said when the truck showed up to deliver all this. Our father stood, hands on his hips, gazing into the truck's back, helplessly bewildered by the burden of what was their history.

What the Jesus fucking goddamn *hell*? she asked him, as if this were a form of existential question.

Our father, an elegant man who doesn't use profanity, gazed into the dark guts of the moving truck and shook his head. He was evidently baffled as to what he was supposed to make of this. He'd been depressed recently. *This* was supposed to cheer him up?

☽

Our father has bright blue eyes and a space between his two front teeth. He is charming, winning, cultivated. That he is also promiscuous will come to me years later from his sister, my aunt, the woman who—aside from my mother—knew and loved my father best. According to Aunt Nan, my father wasn't particularly well equipped for the life he led. He roamed, yet suffered for it. Suffered, then roamed again.

He is so devotedly atheistic that he can find no spiritual avenue, not the road that would bring him home to us, not the one that will take him away for good. The religion practiced in our household is Freudian psychoanalysis, in which confession is offered on a daily basis without either resolution or absolution at the end.

Our parents met at UC Berkeley during the Second World War, when the only men left on campus were those who had enough wrong with them to have been classified 4-F. There was nothing physically wrong with our father. He was tall, dark-haired, blue-eyed, tan from sailing. He was handsome and he was charming. Where my mother was loud and strident, he was soft-spoken, often offering a wry comment half-humorously and sotto voce.

Your father was always *highly* attractive, my mother will say, and always adds, to *both* women and men. She says this as she says most things, in a tone laden with irony, but I know she admires his beauty. It is as if our father's being good looking is just another of her life's own amazing miracles, like their shared artistic talent or the physical beauty of their own three children.

Our grandparents tell my brothers and me over and over again that what is wrong with our parents is that they've always indulged their *artistic* natures, that they chose the wrong friends at Cal, friends who were funny looking and leftist. That my parents imagine they can live outside the rules, as *bohemians*. That my parents have little regard for consequence. We were very small when the chorus began speaking to us like this, in a tone of diagnosis, the ominous shadow of penalty hanging over our uncombed heads.

We endure a double dose of what is wrong with each of them: their promise, their brilliance, their high IQs, their complete lack of common sense. They are intellectually arrogant, the two of them positively convinced they are the two most interesting people either has ever met.

They harbor antisocial attitudes.

And we are their inheritors, our more conventional relatives tell us; they warn us that we are going to have to keep a sharp lookout for our own wayward tendencies. This is also told to us by our grandparents, who are educated and collect art, who love books, music. This confuses me—aren't books and music *artistic*? I eventually figure out that the problem isn't that our parents are *artistic*. It is that they get caught being that.

Others in the family present as more upright, normal: bankers, teachers, the prosperous owner of a building supply company, a consular officer posted to various oil-producing countries. One uncle shocked the family a few years ago by going beneath his *class* in marrying the woman who had been his secretary; she was pregnant when they married. Marriages in our family aren't normally made like this. You don't marry people randomly, and the women are always educated. A woman might even work, as long as it is agreed that it is economically unnecessary.

Our mother's working is not only necessary, it is being practiced with an ever more thinly veiled desperation. *Where is all their money going?* I wonder. Our parents are both *highly neurotic,* as is openly said. I've known words like *neurotic, psychotic, Miltown,* and *breakdown* since before I learned to read. Each is in psychoanalysis, which means driving to West Los Angeles and lying on a psychiatrist's couch four or five times a week, then giving him every cent they ever hoped to make, plus more from their parents, something their parents are not going to ever allow them to ever forget. This huge expenditure is thought to be the fee to purchase what the 1950s promises to people like my parents: happiness, prosperity, normalcy. Our parents' two analysts are discussed so much and so intimately, they seem to me to be invisible members of our own nuclear family.

〇〇〇

My parents look out of the plate-glass window of what will be their final Slumgullion Dream Shack and drink. They drink, they smoke, they say wry things to each other, talking back and forth in code or shorthand, a volley no one else is in on, their words, half joking, only partly said, as one will leave off at what the other is left to finish. They say, We started out with such high hopes, only to find ourselves living next door to Tony and Sylvia Castanzo—Tony, whose job is *itinerate knife sharpening*; Sylvia, who is *always pregnant*. They call the Castanzos *The Dynamic Duo. Big She, Little He. The Psychopathologies of Everyday Life.*

My parents write and paint, each with little to show for it. Each is in *conflict* about what my mother ironically refers to in the singular as their *identity*, as if their twin identities were something they share spiritually. They do seem intimate in a way that transcends language.

It is a terrible time and place for a family like ours. HUAC is in its heyday. In the infant suburbs of postwar Los Angeles everyone is actively afraid of differences. You can See Spot Run. My brothers and I are sometimes taunted at school because we are smart and because our last name, which has a *burgh* at the end, apparently proves that we are Jewish. We are teased because our father wears a suit and tie to work, because that shows we think we are better'n everybody else on our street.

We don't, do we? I ask my mother. We don't think we're better than everybody else.

On Avenue B? my mother says. Oh, yes, we most certainly do.

◊◊◊

My mother hates Huey, Dewey, and Louie, so she quits Disney and takes other awful jobs. For a while she goes door-to-door in high heels and her outdated suits from San Francisco, surveying housewives on the contents of their kitchen cabinets. She can be charming and persuasive when she wants to be. She talks her way inside housewives' front doors, gets them to let her open their refrigerators and their cupboards to do a tabulated inventory. Then they get busy together to mix up little test packets of what will become the first salad dressings and sauces to be marketed as *convenience* foods. She teaches French at a private school, hired on the basis of her fake French accent. Finally she becomes so desperate that she goes back to Disney. She spends even longer hours at the kitchen table, spilling beer and coffee on the Bristol board, flipping her cigarette ashes into empty cans of Pabst Blue Ribbon, talking to Sylvia Castanzo, to me, to anyone who'll listen about how she's noticed that these *ducks* have whole elaborate outfits, shirts and shoes and hats, but *none of them owns any underpants!*

She is drinking heavily by now, and our father has been arrested again. He is arrested for being in *certain bars*. One is called The Lighthouse; it is on the water in Hermosa Beach, where jazz is played. *Certain people* go there—black men, white men, men who might not yet have begun to refer to themselves as "gay." Going to these bars is against the law. I don't yet know why.

He gets arrested even though he is a man incapable of committing a real crime.

Whenever my father is arrested, his psychiatrist, her psychiatrist, his parents, and her parents all talk on the phone, or else meet to confer: Whatever to do about Johnny *this time*?

Call it crime or call it disease—these are the two answers to the question that shouldn't have actually been asked in the first place. But it is finally decided that he needs treatment, so he's sent off to a sanitarium. The logic goes like this: He is married and he has three children, so he can't be a *real* homosexual—perhaps it is something adolescent, something he hasn't outgrown?

So he'll be gone to the hospital that is out in the desert near Palm Springs, or he'll be gone to Mexico, which has a different attitude toward men and masculinity. It was to Mexico his family had always gone on summer holidays, where he was free to be himself, my mother says, where he lived with La Señora, where he practiced his Spanish, admired the new architecture, despised the old neoclassical colonial buildings. Where he wasn't persecuted for being the man he was born to be.

Then he'll come home again, rehabilitated. He'll go back to work, and then he'll be gone again, flying on business out of Los Angeles Airport on a prop plane to Texas or Chicago.

One postcard he sends us from a business trip shows the exterior of the Palmer House in Chicago, an X etched in ink on the high window of the room in which he is staying, maybe measuring the drop.

He is tall, broad faced, freckled, lean, always smiling. He stands at his drafting table, which is shoved into one corner of the already crowded bedroom, smiling hard, as if it hurts his face somewhat to do so. He is working on a house that he says our family will go live in and be happy in. He is a disciple of Wright, of Lescaze, of Neutra, and this ultramodern structure he is drawing looks to me like the shape of a box kite laid on its side on the ground. It is the sort of thing about which my mother will invariably remark, Oh, how *très* ultra-ultra!

One wing is for the adults; the other is designed for the three of us, my brothers and me—they call us *the poor, the huddled, the great unwashed*—to go be unruly in. The connecting struts—the long sides of the box—are solid and walled on the outside, then tiled in waxed flagstone so our wet feet won't mark them. The long halls, with sliding glass that opens onto the interior patio, will be hung with artwork done by our parents and their abnormal Berkeley friends. The outdoor pool in the open center of the house is enclosed on all sides. This, our father says, is so our mother will be able to sunbathe naked. Oh, my darling baby, she tells him when she hears this, arching an eyebrow to say it's he who'd be the one more likely to lay his lanky body out on a chaise, naked in the sunshine, facedown, his dark head cradled on his folded arms, while she stands in the doorway, eyeing him wryly. She'd be turbaned, wearing stylish sunglasses, covered from neck to toe in some smart wrap made of turquoise terry cloth.

He is a better cook than our mother is, but she is a better painter. She recently painted our mailbox in oils, in an abstract expressionist design unappreciated by the neighbors. There are gem cubes that resemble blobs of Jell-O, a huge anti-Disney eye or two, curves and squiggles, black-bordered areas of oceanic blues and greens. The block letters, each stranger and more cubist than the last, spell out THE VANDENBURGHS, which you can read only if you already know what it says. The whole of the mailbox is painted, each inch, and small clay objects have been placed inside to activate its magic, my mother says. The galvanized steel box is covered in paint, and so is the wooden post it sits upon curbside, and even the used-to-be-red sweep-up flag.

That! our grandfather Virgil thunders when he sees it, *no longer conforms to postal regulations.*

2

The Pull of Gravity

IT'S THE WINTER they put Sputnik up. I am nine years old. Our father is gone. He is supposed to be traveling for business in Philadelphia, but he is actually in the desert in a private sanitarium, which is what they call the kinds of mental hospitals that cost a lot of money.

He is there because of LAPD Vice, because of his being arrested again, because of his *acting up*, because of the bribes my grandfather paid to keep him out of jail, because he's cracked up again, as my mother says. When our father is arrested, the captain in Vice calls my paternal grandfather in Glendale. Grandfather John is prominent in building and construction. He goes down to the jail and pays what amounts to a bribe so my father won't go on to be booked and have a record, which would cost him his job.

My grandfather pays the bribe and my father is diverted into the Mental Health side of things. He has to take a leave of absence from work and he's sent out into the desert for months on end, to rest.

That's not what they tell people, though. My mother lies easily; she says he is in Philadelphia, or Dallas, *Texas*, or Houston, *Texas*.

Houston and Dallas are only now being invented, but our mother already despises them, hates Texas, hates anywhere Becket, who is our father's boss, wants to send him to make another city. It is Welton Becket *and Associates*, our mother says, who is responsible for building the same ugly place Los Angeles is turning out to be. Like Mr. Disney's Tomorrowland, it is crappy, tinny, junky.

Becket's offices are on the Miracle Mile, right next to the La Brea Tar Pits. When we drive down Wilshire to take our dad to work, he shudders as we pass beneath the shadows of the new glass-faced office buildings—it's his half-fake shudder, at once real and not real. These are skyscrapers walled with mirrors that mirror nothing. "I will work there until I die," he said one day, which he then very literally did.

But now he's away, so our mother dresses up. She's taking us to dinner at a fish place on the Rainbow Pier. This pier is where my brothers and I hang out on weekends, on school days too. We're now so conspicuous in our truancy that Mr. Loss, the truant officer, knows where to come to look for us. He finds us fishing for bonita, eating saltwater taffy. Mr. Loss piles us in his car and brings us not to school, since we're barefoot and in our bathing suits, but home to our mom. He drives us to our house because, as our mother says, Mr. Loss is a sad, sad little man. Still, she will sometimes ask him in for a breakfast beer. She'll be painting in oils, using one of our dad's white dress shirts as a smock, sleeves rolled up, turned around and buttoned backward.

Her hair is curly, light brown streaked with gold. She doesn't go to the beauty shop to get it *done*, like the other mothers do. Instead, she wears it any way she wants to, long and down in defiance of the fashion or piled up on top of her head, kept there with pencils, paintbrushes, chopsticks, whatever's around for her to stick in it.

Will says Mr. Loss has a *thing* for her. I have no idea what this thing might be.

The place she takes us to is what our mother calls one dump of a jukey joint—the lobster and crab are local; everything is cheap. She sashays in, leading the three of us, orders the first of what she calls her Plural Martinis. Men come around, try to talk to her. Will's seething, challenging, snarling. She very elaborately brushes these men off, saying, I am *married*, but even if I were not, my dear . . . You? *You*? You very obviously do not 'ave enough money for me . . . "

She says the last piece in her fake French accent and turns away.

Never apologize, never explain, she whispers to herself.

Then, to the three of us, she instructs, When a stranger speaks to you, you simply look at him directly and speak slowly and distinctly. You must enunciate clearly. This is what you're to say: I'm-sorry-but-I-do-not-speak-English.

Whatever person was hanging around us until this moment now skulks away; she watches with withering scorn. Then she arches her ironic eyebrow at the hardened starfish twisted into the fishnet that drapes the ceiling, flicks her ash into the abalone shell that's set out for this purpose, and says, only a little too loudly, You'll note, my special darlings, Jukey Joe's clever use of the *seasick* theme?

She's tall, and thin to the point of being bony. She's lately losing interest in what she calls The More Mundane—that we get to school on time, that we go to school at all, that any of us eat. But her attitude toward what she calls *all that* is to remain upbeat, comic, jokey. She's thin, she says, because she's lost her appetite, and *who wouldn't*, she asks, *what with* . . . ?

She gestures around with her cigarette, as if pointing out what's wrong with the tip of her strangely glowing object in the dimness of what is really a cocktail lounge, pointing out *This* and *That* and *That Too*.

Her suits, already out of date, are now too big. These are silk or woolen, tweedy, used-to-be stylish. They were bought in San Francisco, which is a more formal city than L.A., she tells us, where she always wore a hat and gloves when they took the train over the bridge from Berkeley to go for dinner and drinks in downtown San Francisco. San Francisco *suited me*, she says. It *suited* your father, too. You don't call it S.F., she adds, as if this is something we three might do.

She looks pointedly and directly at *me*, as if she has discovered that I am the disloyal one and have actually been thinking I somehow know *better* than she, thinking that I will dare to say *S.F.* even though she has told us not to. It is a piece of my mother's craziness that she can read minds.

This is a dinner Geo, who has just turned five, will not eat because it is lobster, which isn't a hamburger and a chocolate milkshake, and is therefore *upchucky, sickening, icky*, or, as our father says, *enough to makes one's bilge rise*. I know Geo has decided not to eat, because he is resting his forehead on the edge of the table and staring down into his upcurled hands that lie open in his lap. When he does this, my parents call it Geo's *praying*, or *keening*, or *acting tragic*.

Ah, well, old boy, our father would say with faux hardiness, all the more for the rest of us. And he'd reach over with his own fork to take what he wanted from Geo's plate.

After dinner we go to the arcade at the foot of the pier, where my mother, my brothers, and I all cram into the photo booth to have our pictures taken, four shots for a quarter. Will wins a plush purple animal, grabbed out of the glass box by the mechanical claw he calls the Sky Hook. This stuffed dog is so inspired in its ugliness, it moves our mother, now being hilarious, to take us to another booth, where we sing into the mic to cut a scratchy record that the machine presses out of bright red plastic and delivers within minutes.

In the playback booth, my mother and I hear ourselves sing in our high, hurt voices that only hover next to notes, while Will self-confidently booms louder so his voice stands in front of ours, as if he's our leader now and is marching us up and down this song's hills and valleys.

Will is thirteen, now taller than our mother, and his voice is lowering gracefully. I hear him singing around the house when he thinks no one's listening. "But no 'tis not a boy at all," he sings, "'tis Axle's castle's spires so tall . . . " This is a song he's learning for glee club. Will is good at singing and at school and at sports, girls like him, he's good at everything. I worry about this because being good at things is both good and bad, because each time we succeed it takes us further from our parents.

Geo's real name is George Charles. They call him Geo, short for Georgio, because—they say—he was conceived in an Italian villa, a beautiful house with terraced gardens and a water course, someplace my parents were house-sitting for rich friends of my father's rich parents. Villa Vino Santo Multo Vino Vino Santo, they call it, a place of vineyards, olive trees, abundance. God knows why they really named him this. I was alive when Geo was born, and I can remember where we lived, and this was a certain apartment in Verdugo Woodlands. It had nothing to do with Italy, which is on the continent of Europe, somewhere I happen to know my mother has never been.

Geo's voice is beautiful, too, as warbling and ethereal, our father says, as one of God's more neutral angels'. Our father often says this kind of dreamy, inscrutable thing. He says Geo sings to the birds in their own language, which is why they follow him home. Geo resembles a certain saint in this, our father says, the one who was too crazy for people to listen to, so he spoke his wisdoms to the birds.

Geo accumulates living things; they accrete to him by magnetism. He has recently brought home a damaged parakeet with only one good leg. He found it wounded in the dirt of the alleyway behind our house. This bird hopped to him, then rode home perched on Geo's finger.

Another time he found a baby finch and took it home wrapped and cradled in the hem of his T-shirt, a bird so small we had to feed it with an eyedropper. Once it was a litter of mongrel pups that arrived in somebody else's wicker laundry basket, meaning Geo probably stole them.

Can we keep them? we begged our father anyway. There were three puppies, one for each of us. And our father was always great about pets; we always got to keep them. He'd get us a puppy or a kitten as a consolation prize anytime anything went wrong—we had countless pets because of it. We got Ziggy because L.A. County outlawed fireworks. Ziggy is short, black, and fattish, and our favorite dog. Anytime we'd get a new pet we'd take it to Olivera Street for the Blessing of the Animals on the Feast Day of Saint Francis of Assisi.

And now we want these puppies. He always says yes, but this time he's different. Not this week, he says. You won't be here this weekend to take care of them. I'm out of town and you're going to the Whites'.

The Whites are my mother's parents. The Whites are *a piece of work*, our mother says, *scary business, hell on wheels*. The Whites *lower the boom* when they're around. The Whites show up and *there's hell to pay*.

Can't we take them to Lina and Virgil's? Please? Please let us have them, please! we beg.

We think he's going to say yes. He always says yes. But this time our father says, I wouldn't take them to the flea circus.

I don't know what a flea circus is, or if a flea circus in fact exists. Does he mean that while he wouldn't take these other people's dogs to a flea circus, he might take them someplace else?

Frankly, our mother says, you show up with a new batch of puppies for my mother to housebreak, and she will *kill herself*. Geo, you need to show Daddy exactly where you got those dogs. She's saying this just as the family with the mother dog arrives on our front porch.

Geo sings out from the speakers in the playback booth, where we're playing the bright red record. "How much is that doggie in the window? The one with the waggedy taaa-aaa-aaail?" Geo is singing with so much feeling and sincerity, it would make the sentimental weep, except that no one in our family is the least bit sentimental. Life has a way of beating sentiment right out of you, our mother says, what *with* . . . ? As we listen to the scratchy record playing back this part of the song, we can also hear the other three of us in the background, laughing softly at Geo's innocence.

The record is part of a gift we're accumulating for our father, for our mother to take to him for us. So far we have a bag of saltwater taffy, the photo strip, the scary purple dog–ish thing, and now this record that we've just made for him. We'll send this package off to him in the desert, then wait for him to come back to us. He will always come back to us, our mother says, because we are irresistible. *Nothing*, no one, has ever come between them, she says, and *nothing* ever will.

We all walk along the beach at the waterline, watching the waves for the shadowy shapes of grunion, the sand for hermit crabs and blobs of jellyfish. We search the sky for Sputnik, which is easily spotted as it blinks across like a dot-dot-dotting star. It resembles an ellipsis, the mark you put on the page to show something's been left out. Our father is an ellipsis, now here, now here, now not. The satellite is beautiful. The only thing wrong with Sputnik is that our enemies put it up.

On the map of the world in my brothers' bedroom, my mother has painted half the countries various shades of red and named them The Domino Effect. Whatever this means, we don't believe in it.

All the *good* relatives—that's what our mother calls her parents, the Whites, also the Ainsworth-Roland-Rutherfords, the Moseses-Vandenburghs-Snowdens—are Republicans, which is why they're afraid of the communists.

If you're a Republican, she says, you talk about how you like Ike and how the commies want to bomb us. If you're a Democrat, you prefer to speak of how the Russian language has written this great literature. It could do this because it has a hundred words for *vodka*, another hundred for *potato*, and a hundred more for *dirt*. Russia is somehow the reason Jewish people in Hollywood have lost their jobs, and our parents know people like this, those said to be *commies, pinkos, reds.*

My mother is wearing a pair of her good high heels, though we're walking on the sand. She takes them off to walk along the waterline. She wears hose, almost never goes barefoot. She wears shoes because she hates na-chur—she is, she says, an admirer of the Great Indoors. She also wears shoes because her father, who was a banker, believes people's character can be judged by the quality of their shoe leather. This is a value her father, whom she calls Virgil *Elmo* White—as if to differentiate him from all the other Virgil Whites who were rattling around in our family—has instilled in her, though this life lesson, she says, is perfect and utter crap.

Listen to me! she'll say in her I'm Giving Instructions voice. Sometimes she'll wake us up in order to Give Instructions. Listen! she'll say to our heavy bodies, struggling to climb out of sleep. This is what your parents do to you! They make you believe all sorts of idiotic stuff, lousy shitty useless things that are in no way true—do you understand me?

We stir and nod and nod, though this makes no sense to us.

Other wisdom she needs to impart is that you do not, for instance, get sick from sitting on a toilet seat. Urine is sterile, she says, which is why soldiers in battle are told to pee on their wounds.

Her banker-giving-loans-on-the-basis-of-your-shoe-leather father is the reason my brothers and I are hardly ever told to put on shoes. We go barefoot because we pretend we're Indians, being raised by these ghostly ancestors who are just so much better than our own. We are Ishi, the last Yahi, and we hide from Mr. Loss in the crumbling sandstone caves that are wave carved and wind carved into the hillside above the beach, where the air is cold and wet and ancient. Ishi is the story our father tells us; he took anthropology at Cal from Kroeber, who was the white man Ishi lived with. Ishi was the last of his people, a real Indian who came down out of the hills near Oroville and walked out of the Stone Age and into the twentieth century.

It is the miracle of our century, our father says, that it started with prehistory and now has Sputnik in it.

More Life Instructions from my mother: You do not get pneumonia from going out with a wet head. If you sneeze three times, a letter will not come, and if you swear—*I swear to God*—God does not fucking launch fucking lightning bolts to strike you dead. If there is a G-a-w-d, which she sincerely doubts, he'd have *much more* important things to worry about than striking people dead over that kind of crappy shit.

We wear bathing suits in all weather; we pull on shorts and sweat-shirts over them. And we wear flip-flops that we call zoris, which our father buys in Chinatown—it's where he gets me tabi socks. Our mother would never wear anything like this. Even in the house, she clomps down the hallway in her high heels to the bathroom in the middle of the night, where there is sometimes blood in the toilet if she forgets to flush it.

∞

What holds it up? Geo asks. He's looking at the wavering dot-dot-dot blinking across the whole huge dome of lesser stars. *Sputnik*, in Russian, means *traveling companion*.

Gravity, Will says shortly, as if Geo's a fool for asking. My older brother tests as a genius in math, science, and language, but being as geniusy as he is, my mother says, is *its own special problem*. It makes a kid impatient, she says. She knows all about this because she was that kind of genius, too. They kept skipping her through the grades, so she graduated from high school when she was barely sixteen and had to stay out for a year before they'd let her into Cal. Her skipping grades accounts, she says, for at least *hawwwwwf* of her social maladaption. The other half being that everything cutesy and girlsie has always bored her to fucking tears.

What's gravity? my little brother asks.

Will breathes out a withering little blast and stares off without answering.

It has to do with forces, I tell Geo. We'll look it up in *Compton's* when we get home, I say. I know gravity has something to do with pull, that it lies in the same realm of whatever force makes iron filings come out of the sand and attach themselves to the ends of magnets so they look drippy and wet.

Forces are what things have that make other things come to them.

Words like *force*, like *vice*, like S-E-X, like *badminton* and *shuttle-cock*, are simply beyond me. I am an ordinary child, and it's too hard to understand or even think about these things without the illustrations that will explain them. This is why I am reading *Compton's Pictured Encyclopedia,* or if not reading then at least looking at it book by book, looking at the pictures, imagining that all this knowledge, when taken together, might yield a better map than the one of the world my mother is doing on the wall of my brothers' bedroom, where many of the countries are painted in strange, un-maplike colors and aren't even named.

History and science are what my family has, because we don't go to church. We don't go to church because we're the branch of the family who are what our father calls *card-carrying atheists*. The California Indians had no maps and only the bare rudiments of a written language, as our father has explained—pictures on rocks and things. Something happens to the mind when you write things down, when you can begin to see the world as an orb observed from above. He thinks about things from above because of his work as an architect.

Geo isn't happy with my answer, so Will relents and bends down, and is now drawing a chart of our solar system with a stick in the hard sand, showing Geo that Sputnik is traveling, like our own moon, in orbit around the earth, and that the stars are farther off.

Then what holds the stars up? Geo asks our mom. Through that pure night air, the stars seem to jiggle and dance, this jitter caused by *atmosphere*.

Why, sweetie-honey-baby, she sighs, I honestly have *no idea*. Then she smirks. She smirks as if she's sharing this joke with our dad, the now-here, now-here, now-not-here, who is what she sometimes calls Your Faw-thur Which Aren't in Heaven. This is how I know she's drunk.

Geo begins to cry.

Wrong answer, Mom, I say. Wrong answer for a five-year-old.

Geo's crying harder now, so our mother kneels on the hard sand and takes him in her lap, singing in her broken voice, Ground-round version, mother and child, holy infant so tender and mild, sleep in heavenly peeeep, sleep in heavenly peep. She sings this though it is February.

There, *there*, there, *there*, she tells Geo, holding him to her, grimacing over his head to go, See! From this Will and I are supposed to get how hilarious it is that our mother is being expected to act like a mother, instead of what she really is, which is this rare thing, this wonderfully gifted and spectacular being, the Radiant Child she has always been.

We carefully pack up each part of my father's present, and on the weekend we go to stay at the Whites' while my mother drives the present out to him, to where he's staying in the desert. She drives in her new car, which is blue and white two-tone, which her father has recently bought. She is supposed to use this car to go back to work at Disney in Burbank, but our mother despises Mr. Disney and plans to go nowhere near the man.

Her car has slanted *OOO*s all along its sides, and when she comes home from the hospital this time, she has my father with her, and he's pale and seems afraid. He stays in bed with a pillow over his face, or gets up in his PJs and moves to the couch. He spends weeks without speaking. He's too fearful to drive a car; he believes the police are following him. When he does drive, it's to go to Blackie's to buy a six-pack of beer; then he stops on the side of the road so he can hide the beer somewhere in the trunk.

We go to the beach with our aunt and uncle and our four cousins, and we're going to play cribbage and put up the badminton net, and we have inner tubes that my dad and my uncle got us from the service station, and it starts out being fun, like in the Olden Days, when things used to be easy and even ordinary, back when my mom and dad and my aunt and uncle were the best of friends.

My aunt has brought my father's favorite kind of sandwich, which is avocado with cut-up green onions and mayonnaise on a kind of bread they call Dutch crunch. I can see how her eyes watch him behind her sunglasses, because my father is her big brother and they've always been the favorite persons of each other, and he's lying on his side in the sand, trying to smile the wide hard smile he's always been able to smile with the gap between his two front teeth, but now he no longer can.

And suddenly he's lying facedown on his towel and my mother's bending over him, and my uncle orders us all to walk down the beach with him and pick up litter, which he calls policing the area, and when we get back my mother and father are gone and my aunt's face is pale behind her tan.

We go home that afternoon with Nan and Ned in their station wagon, seven kids lying in the back, sunburned and sandy. We stay with them in the Valley at least through the weekend, and my cousin Graham and I sleep in the same bed, with our heads on pillows at opposite ends, but we kick each other and fight, so my aunt moves me into Lizzie's room.

My mother tells us later our father had a sunstroke. I've begun to dream that he is drowning and that I'm on the cliff above the sea where the caves are carved below and I cannot get down to him and I know I cannot save him. This dream makes no sense, since he's an expert swimmer who grew up sailing his own little skiff from the pier at Hermosa near his parents' beach house, and it is he who has taught me to swim in the ocean. I dream I see the shape of his body in the waves as they rise up, the sun gleaming through so it shows in silhouette, then see the shape dissolving as it twists and swirls and comes apart as grains of sand.

My parents call their psychiatrists Dr. Maudlin and Dr. Moody. We sometimes wait in the car, reading comic books and chewing Black Jack gum, while our mother's seeing her psychiatrist.

My father sees his psychiatrist every day of the week on his lunch hour. This is Dr. Mailin, whose office is up the street from Becket, near Bullock's Wilshire. An accident of history has placed my father, a couple of days a week, riding up or riding down in the same elevator as Marilyn Monroe, whose own psychiatrist, Dr. Ralph Greenson, has an office down the hall from Mailin's. She wears no makeup, keeps a scarf over her hair, and wears huge sunglasses, and she and my father very carefully ignore each other, each recognizing the other as fragile and distraught.

Dr. Mailin approves of my father's flirtations with good-looking women—and my father does flirt with women, and sometimes even goes off with them—because this is a "boysie" thing to do. What LAPD Vice does not approve of is my dad's flirting with good-looking men.

One of the more important pieces of advice my parents' psychiatrists have given them is that my father must begin to act more "boysie" and my mother must start to act more "girlsie." Toward the aim of my father's acting boysie, his psychiatrist orders him to start doing more typically fatherly things, to work on being the kind of man any father would like his boys to grow up to be—less of a hanging-out-in-bars father, more of a hunting-and-fishing one. He is to take my brothers camping, and only the boys can go. Fathers Camping with Sons is evidently the way people act in other, more normal families.

I am shocked when I hear this plan, too hurt and astonished to even cry. Instead, I take the kitchen scissors into the bathroom and cut off all my hair. My hair is blond and curly, it is Shirley Temple hair, it is one of the major things Will makes fun of me for. Now it's gone. With my hair cropped close, I dress in his jeans, put on his Keds and ball cap, and shove myself into the backseat of my father's car, hold on to the armrest, and scream that they will never get me out of the car, that they will never never never make me stay home.

They pull me out and drive to Lake Piru, which my father tells me later is just this *hole in the wall.*

I am left alone in the house with my mother for the weekend, and while it's my father who has been sent camping for his mental health, it's my mother who is insane, as I have always known.

Meanwhile, my father's life on Earth is ending, and though we don't know this, we still sense time going faster in the way it will when a story is winding itself up, when all the events begin to crowd in and collide, in order that each has a chance to decree itself, and they compete in getting themselves told.

And now my parents are being ordered by their psychiatrists to take us to Disneyland, though they both hate this kind of thing, though he is too depressed to speak, to lift his head. Inside the park he sits on a bench, holding his arms as if they ache, waits as we joylessly stand in line. I refuse to have fun out of loyalty to him. The only ride I will go on is Peter Pan, which is beautiful, which shows the lights of London far below, and I think about being able to fly one day out a window and far above the lights of Earth, and that I'd be certain to take my brothers and our dog and leave nobody behind. Wendy and her Lost Boys.

But time has now become foreshortened and oppressed, and my brothers and I finally become so inoculated by the sodden hopelessness that we, too, turn quiet and no longer beg for anything. We've become such good children, it is as if we've learned to behave. We are the ones who sit in the backseat on the drive home with our empty hands up-turned in our laps. We ride along in silence, and maybe it is this new quiet of ours that speaks to the quiet in our father, because when we pass a carnival alongside the highway, he pulls over, stops the car, and takes us on the Ferris wheel, that one last time.

3
Thirty-Six Miles

IT'S A WEDNESDAY in February. Our mom keeps us home from school and makes Will and me stay in, though she lets Geo out to play. The phone rings, then rings again. We have only one phone, which is in the hallway between the living room and the kitchen. We can hear it ring and the murmuring of her voice, but not any of the words she's saying.

Will and I are playing chess in my mother and father's bedroom. I play with Will, also with my Grandfather Virgil, though I'm never allowed to win. My family is harsh like this—you don't get to win because you're younger or don't know how to play, and especially not because you are a girl.

We are sitting on the huge mahogany bed our dad got from his grandmother. This kind of furniture came Round the Horn, our mother says. Your faw-thur's family, she says, came to California by ship and train, while the little girls in her family, like Perseus Bartholomew and America Orchard, got behind the ox cart and walked. This is to make some point I have never understood, about the difference in class between their two very similar families. I hate thinking about these things.

The Oregon Trail, the people who did or didn't come west by walking two thousand miles, bores me in a particularly headachy way. It's the same as having to watch some educational movie in school or a stupid filmstrip on a hot day with the blinds down, the motes being all I can concentrate on. I hate cowboy-and-Indian movies for this same reason, for the long shots of dry, dusty landscapes in which there is no town as far as you can see, and the whole thing is done to show the puny plume of smoke that is the dust cloud blooming up behind the tiny horse and even tinier rider.

I already get the insignificance of Man Against the Elements. The thought of these things fills me with the kind of terrifying loneliness and existential dread I imagine my father feels.

My mother comes into the bedroom and stands framed in the doorway, holding one arm to her side in the rigid way she has. Children, she says, your father committed suicide this morning.

I cry out, I scream, I am doubled over weeping. My mother flinches. My brother is embarrassed by my reaction—they both hate it when anyone is being what they call *emotional*. Neither of them cries; neither says much of anything, except to say I need to calm down, that we need to plan and put this plan into action.

She tries to hold me in her arms, but I shrug her off and climb through my parents' oversize and crowded-together bedroom furniture to stand in the window behind the headboard, sobbing into my own hands.

My mother hands me one of my father's handkerchiefs. I bring it to my face and begin to sob harder because it smells like him.

The morning is whitening. The sky carries the particular yellowish color of the light reflected off the sandy soil of our back lot, which has never been planted. My mother and brother are asking me to come out, saying I have to stop crying, that we have to go find Geo. We need to pack our animals and drive across the L.A. Basin to the Whites'.

Why? I ask. *I'm not going with her*, I think. *I'm staying here to wait for my father to get home.*

In that moment, I hate my mother as intensely as I did on the weekend I was left home with her while the boys went camping at Lake Piru. We were *supposed* to do girlsie things while they were away, which—to my mother—meant we *would not clean house, would not shop, would not wear an apron.* She dressed up, put on makeup, took her daughter, and went to the Rainbow Pier, where I sat next to her on a barstool, drinking ginger ale with cherries in it while she drank martoonies and ranted about how the psychiatrists of the state of California were engaged in this conspiracy that involved the Vice Squad of the Los Angeles Police Department.

I don't ask her how he died, because I don't actually believe that he has. I am reframing the events linguistically, telling myself he attempted suicide but failed, as my parents have so determinedly failed at everything else they've tried.

He attempted suicide, I keep saying to myself.

You're going to have to stop crying, my brother says. It's upsetting Mom.

But I will not. *I will never stop crying*, I think. *The two of them can't make me. They have no way of understanding what I've lost. They're not crying because they still have each other, but it was my father who approved of me. Now I have no one but Geo and my dog.*

The manner of my father's death is nothing anyone wants to discuss, so I don't find out how he died until several days after. I imagine ways he's died—driving our mom's car off a cliff into the sea, for instance. I imagine. I don't ask.

But later that week, my mother and I drive home from Glendale to pack up some things we need—the house will be sold, we'll never live in Redondo again. When we get there there are newspapers collected all around the front porch. I open them until I get to the one that was published the morning after my father's death, and I begin to read.

It says he jumped off the roof of his office building into the parking lot.

〰

It is years later, after I become an adult, when I finally talk to my father's friend Peter DiFrenzi, who walked with him that morning at the La Brea Tar Pits. My father was gloomy and markedly anxious. He'd tried calling his doctor time and time again, but the psychiatrist had yet to call back, as Peter told my mother when he phoned her on the morning of my father's death. Peter'd also called my grandmother and my father's sister, whose husband phoned the doctor and threatened him with bodily injury.

You're a quack, my uncle said.

Though he and Peter had already gone out walking earlier that morning, my father gathered up his coat from the hanger where he kept it, saying he guessed he needed to get some air.

My father worked standing at his drafting table, which faced that of Peter. They both worked in their shirtsleeves. On that day, my father rolled down his sleeves and buttoned the cuffs, then put on his coat, saying he was going on a coffee break.

Some coffee break, my mother liked to say.

〰

The day our father dies, we have to gather up our animals to take them in the car to go to our grandparents' house. When we get there, things will be better because Dr. Greenly is coming to give our mother a sedative, but first she has to drive us there, so she can't crack up quite *yet*.

She has decided that Will and I can know, but that Geo, who doesn't know what the word *suicide* means, is too young to understand, so we aren't to discuss this with him, which also keeps us from saying anything about what has happened. We tell Geo our father has gone away on a business trip, so we're going to Lina and Virgil's for a while. This makes him happy because he's Lina's favorite person.

Ziggy is riding shotgun. He has short legs but no sense at all that he's small. He's my favorite dog because he's happy and self-confident. We always get mutts from the pound because our father says they're more well adjusted.

My brothers and I ride in the backseat, holding our other pets. Will and I are at either window; Geo is in the middle, with his hermit crabs' terrarium on his lap.

Will has these friends named Norman and Yvonne Fisher who live across the street and down the block. They are a brother and sister about a year apart in age. Norman and Yvonne miss as much school as we do, so Mr. Loss knows them, too. It's because their parents are separated and their mother works. The only other woman who works a steady job in our neighborhood is Ann, of Bud and Ann next door. Because they don't have children, it's whispered that Ann has something wrong with her *parts*.

The Fishers are worse kids than even the Vandenburghs, so wild and truant that Maxine Woodman calls them Bad-Uns. Will told me it was at the house of Norman and Yvonne Fisher that the neighborhood kids a little older than I am established a sex club. This is like, I'm guessing, the pigeon club we've had as a semi-organized activity, with parental support, that Will has recently outgrown.

I've read *Where Babies Come From*, so I know what sex is and am not surprised that Norman Fisher's involved, as he's already famous for his proto-perversions, his bragging that he can suck his own balls or his peeing into a milk bottle that's half filled with water, his demanding that little kids drink a sip of it before they're allowed into the Fishers' house, which is something I don't do, because that place is somewhere I don't actually want to go.

Norman and Yvonne are lurking in their side yard as we go back and forth to pack our car. They're stooping to pick up some green fruit that lies around a tree, throwing it hard against the stucco wall of their house, but also watching us. As we close the car doors and begin to take off, they start toward the street, peering in to make sure Will's in here with us. Our mom hasn't really accelerated yet and is only letting the car roll downhill in neutral, as if she can't quite remember how to drive.

She brakes as she pulls over on the wrong side of the road, stopping next to the Fishers' mailbox, which sits on a post by the curb. Yvonne wanders out, moving hips-first in a sultry way that is already knowing and seductive.

Can Will come over and play, Mrs. Vandenburgh? she asks. She is leaning over to peer into our car, curious about why we're traveling with all our animals.

Our mother is smoking, her left arm dangling out the window. She catches my eye in the rearview mirror and arches an eyebrow ironically, as if to say, See? Even on an extraordinary day such as today, you can count on Yvonne to act so totally *Yvonne.*

Not today, dear, my mother says.

She waits and purses her lips in a certain way she has, as if she's thinking about trying the punch line out on Yvonne. It will become, over the years, our most riotous and cosmic joke. It becomes our tagline, our appositive, that without which we are no longer ourselves, as it defines us away from the world in which we did once live.

Will can't play today, our mother says. His father has *committed suicide.*

And later I'll understand that she'll have to say it over and over again in order to believe it, because we still could not believe it, would never really quite believe it, so we say this to people, then watch their faces for shock or horror or pity, as if—if it did turn out to be true—their expressions might give us a hint of what we are supposed to feel.

Yvonne lets out a little yelp, like she's been stung by a bee, and her eyes immediately fill, which bothers my mom. Crying always bothers my mother because she never cries herself.

Oh, there, *there,* dear, she says to Yvonne, though she is no longer paying very close attention. Buck up, dear, we all must buck up now, mustn't we? she says, but she isn't looking at Yvonne. Instead, she is fiddling with the rearview mirror. We're in the Nash, so everything needs adjustment, as she is only that moment noticing.

Everything needs adjustment because our father, who was so tall, was the last one to drive this car. This day he's evidently driven our mother's new blue and white one to the office.

Our mother sighs hugely, theatrically, at the arduousness of everything, *what with* . . . ? She examines the expression on her face in the mirror on the sun visor, sucks her cheeks in, then flips the visor up. Her face is focused and plain as she presses her foot to the accelerator.

She is steering carefully, concentrating on driving us safely down the road. She drives us from Redondo Beach north, along the Harbor

Freeway and through downtown, then up into the foothills that stand between Glendale and Flintridge, then up Montecito, then down over the culvert and onto Vista del Mar to our grandparents' house. It is thirty-six miles. It is the hardest thing she will ever do.

They are outside waiting for us. She gets out of the car and falls down in the middle of the street.

4
The Salisbury Court Reporter

AFTER MY FATHER steps forward, falls six stories, and disappears, my mother finishes going crazy. She buys a new house with a bomb shelter, a gold Naugahyde sofa bed, a black-and-white kidney-shaped coffee table, Johnny Mercer albums. She calls everyone she knows long-distance and talks for hours.

We move to a new house that has a pomegranate tree, on a street called Salisbury Court. We have two birds: a parakeet named Perky and a finch named Pickering, after the colonel on the *My Fair Lady* album, where the record sticks, going, Pickering, Pickering, Pickering. Our mother is crazy now, so we all need to attend to this kind of magical underscore, certain patterns and repetitions that here and there emerge. There is algebraic significance to these sets of threes and sevens—also to the appearances of dogs and birds and various saints.

Perky is a broken yellow parakeet with one lame foot that is curled into an unnatural shape, some imperfect mark of punctuation. He is flawed, so Perky is, of course, our favorite. Geo is the one who found him. Geo, who has always been silent, is witchy now; like St. Francis, he speaks only to the animals now, so that's how they find him. Perky dies, or flies away, after a few weeks in the new house.

The finch flies freely in the house until it drowns in the dishwater in the kitchen sink. My brothers and I fish the wet bird out, then bury him in a shoebox under the dirt floor of the bomb shelter, this cold, damp, concrete-smelling alcove. We have a bomb shelter because this is the 1950s and everyone is afraid of communists. Our mother believes in a conspiracy that has to do with how our parents had been Leftists in college, but not, evidently, Leftist enough. You could never be the right kind of Leftist, our mother says, and this is the reason, evidently, that now the commies are after us.

The conspiracy accounts for the absence of our father, who either is or isn't dead, according to the degree of her craziness, which is in perpetual flux. The conspiracy is intricate. It involves Russia, electronic surveillance, each and every psychiatrist either of our parents has ever seen, including a psychiatric social worker whose name is Marge le Farge or, variously, Marge the Barge de Farge, and also the operators at the telephone company at Ninth and Hope in downtown Los Angeles, who have now begun to listen in on our mother's phone conversations.

She knows about the conspiracy because her French professor laid it all out for her in drabs of dusty chalk on the blackboard when she was at Cal. It took the form of a mathematical equation involving an Unknown Quantity. Our father was an Unknown Quantity, she said—neither This-nor-That, but rather Both-And, and so, she said, were we. We three were also Other.

If we were filling out a form, she instructed us, we were to write down *Other* when we were asked to say what we were.

Our father was better at math than she was, but she is the better writer. But she understands the arithmetic of the conspiracy—the French professor had explained it to her because he'd been in love with her. And he wasn't the only one, she reminds us. Seven men asked her to marry them, though her underwear was dirty. Do we understand her? she asks. Do we understand exactly what she is alluding to?

We nod, but we have no idea what she is talking about, except that it probably has something to do with what she calls *S-E-X*.

She has proof of the plot against her in that there are cars driving past our house in sets of threes. Her psychiatrist is the one in the red-orange VW, see? And it is being driven by his right-hand man, Marge the Barge de Farge, and when our mother calls her his right-hand *man*, she says, she is using the term advisedly.

I never see this car, but still I nod with my brothers and act as if I get her jokes, the one about Marge being his right-hand man and so forth. I know this is a joke the way our new house is a joke: She chose it because Salisbury Court was a dead-end street.

Dead. End. Street. Words like these now come freighted with all kinds of important meaning. *Dead-end street* now rhymes, in our mother's musical, comedic mind, with *sets of threes* and with *Pickering.*

∞

Without my mother's aid or governance, my brothers and I make up schedules for ourselves that we then struggle to follow. We have a meeting every Sunday, when the program guide comes out, to vote on television programs for the week. Will calls this meeting to order. He also instructs Geo on various matters of etiquette and propriety, telling him, for instance, that he has to finish his carrots and his peas.

Why? Geo asks.

Because you have to.

Why? Geo asks again. Daddy says I don't have to. Daddy says, All the more for the rest of us.

Said, Will tells him. *Daddy said*, but Geo just stares away. Geo's face is tanned, sunburned, freckled all at once, the individual hairs so blond they look glassy and transparent, eyes so blue they are like turquoise marbles in the mahogany game Grandmother Delia has on her coffee table that her father brought from China, marbles that are speckled and swirled with layers of golden iridescence.

Just eat them, Will says.

Will also tries to help our mother budget her money, which seems to have descended upon us in an incomprehensible blizzard. He once looked up from the mess that was her big-as-a-photo-album checkbook—this was a checkbook out of Dickens, really, and it had elaborate ledgers on which to do complicated double-entry accounting. Her father, who was a banker, was the person responsible for her having this ridiculous account, with its black and pebbled self-important cover and its checks set up three to a page that you needed to tear out carefully along their rigorous lines of microperforations. These were huge, like comic-book checks, and Will was now regularly signing our mother's name.

He glanced up and asked, Hey, Mom, why can't you be a more regular mom, like the one on *Leave It to Beaver*?

A *Leave It to Beaver* mother? our mother asked. As opposed to the kind I *really* am, which is the Queen of the Fucking May?

She loves Will particularly well, so he is permitted to say this kind of thing to her, which coming from me might sound like less of an observation and more of a criticism.

The huge, official-looking checkbook is a joke and the telephone is a joke and the bill that the telephone company sends us is another of the jokes in this portion of our lives, which—to our mother—have begun to resemble some grimly comedic light opera in which our father flew from the roof of a building and won't reappear until a later act.

Will opens the telephone bill. He says that it is more than $300.

She talks on the phone all night, every night, while Geo has now stopped speaking almost entirely. It is nearly summer, so Will has arranged to have Geo go to the Talako Club, which is for all the rich little boys and girls. Will is doing these things now, as our mother seems unable to. But she says Geo needs to learn to swim and ride horseback like all of the other rich little boys and girls of La-Dee-Da La Cañada-Flintridge. We are in disguise now, our mother says, as rich little boys and girls. She's hidden us among the rich because the rich are almost always safer.

Will keeps getting into fights at school. When he gets caught, the principal calls my mother to come and get him. I am home one day when this happens. I stay home because I don't want to go to school, where I have no friends, or sometimes I have friends but I don't like them because they aren't the friends I used to have when we lived in Redondo. I stay home because my mother wants me with her, as if we're in this together, and she talks to me like I'm her confidante.

I watch her ready herself in the bathroom mirror. It's always theatrical, as if she's getting herself into costume for her role in some play. She splashes her face with baby oil, pouts, draws on lips. She is wearing huge dark glasses and, in the fashion of the times, has her hair wrapped in a terry-cloth turban. She is tall and is now thinner than she's ever been. She's stopped eating, preferring, she says, to get most of her vitamins and essential nutrients from the hops and grains and barley in Pabst Blue Ribbon, which is—as everybody knows—one of Nature's Most Perfect Foods.

When the principal calls again, our mother sighs hugely and then goes to meet him. She has a new motto now, which is Public Opinion No Longer Worries Me, which she got from a *New Yorker* cartoon that she's taped to the wall. It has a Gahan Wilson monster: warty, three-eyed, hugely deformed, surrounded by beautiful people at a cocktail

party. The monster is sipping a drink. "Public opinion," he is saying
urbanely, "no longer worries me." This is why she drives the car dead
drunk, wearing what she is wearing, which is high heels and her bathing
suit, her hips draped with a bright red floral sarong.

I am in the fifth grade, but I don't go to school very often, and I have
no friends there. One time a girl, whose last name is really normal—
something Normal! Normal! Normal! as my mother says, flashing her
fingers open and shut like her hands are a warning signal—invites me
to spend the night. This girl's father is a minister, and the entire family
sits around the table after dinner—guided by the Reverend Smith or
Jones—to talk to me about sins on my soul. They keep a Bible sitting diagonally on a table in the corner; I try not to look at it, but its gilt edges
shine out in a manner that feels inevitable. I understand that a Bible is a
perfectly ordinary, everyday object in the lives of other people, but it is
completely terrifying to me—that or anything else that seems to reek of
any kind of religiosity, any kind of potent relic. I think this Bible might
burst into flames if you hold it, or that if you open its cover you'll find it
to be a literal portal to a literal hell from which live snakes might begin
to writhe and crawl.

I fall asleep that night with bubble gum in my mouth and wake the
next morning with my face stuck to the pillowcase. I know they will never ask me back. It doesn't matter. My father was an atheist and I am an
atheist. My mother was an atheist, too, until she started hearing voices.

My favorite show is *I Led Three Lives*. My favorite singer is Harry
Belafonte. Someone has given me a miniature printing press with rubber letters, so I start a newspaper called *The Salisbury Court Reporter*.
I watch, I listen. I begin to practice the plain dumb blank face that is
the pretend neutralness of journalism. I begin to write in an infinitely
neat and exacting manner, forming block letters that are tiny, miraculously precise. *It is an architect's hand*, I think, *one that I've never*

learned, but here is my father's own printing that has been magically bequeathed to me.

I write down the *pointedly average,* the usual, the friendly, the news that everyone wants to hear. I have a specialty that is the human-interest story that shows some mild ironic twist. What I don't put in is anything about what is going on at our house, where the four or six or even eight of us—if you count birds and dogs and ghosts—exist in this hypertheatrical manner that our mother now seems to believe is being stage-directed by some perversely unfunny god.

What I don't put in is that our mother has buried her new car in the garage, beneath hundreds and hundreds of beer cans. She is hiding her beer cans in the garage. She is hiding her cans from the neighbors, the communists, the psychiatrists, and our grandparents.

Her fear is new. In Redondo she'd been afraid of no one. She'd been a porch drinker, who refused, on goddamned principle, to pour her beer into a civilized glass. She drank from the can on purpose, in defiance of the etiquette of the time, of being all nicey-nice or Too Goddamnned Girlsie for Words.

In Redondo, my mother would not be nice, she would not be girlsie. She'd sit on the concrete of our house at the beach with her long arms wrapped around herself against the chill of the late afternoon, drinking a beer, smoking a cigarette. Maxine Woodman, who was hugely fat, was the boss of our neighborhood, but our mother wasn't afraid of her. Maxine would trundle herself uphill from where she'd been, which was down the street meddling. She puffed as she walked, scuffed in her slippers and housecoat out in the middle of the street. She walked in the street because she was from the country, our mother said, which made her an Oakie or Arkie.

Been drinking, Margaret? she'd ask as she puffed uphill.

Been eating, Maxine? our mother would say right back.

◎

I don't put in my paper the perhaps newsworthy item that both toilets in our house are broken and none of us seemingly has the wit or guile to call the plumber. We either can't or won't, but anyway we haven't, and the toilet will not fix itself. Things do not get better by themselves. Instead, we simply come to a new low in this new Slumgullion, to which we've been perplexingly assigned and to which we are becoming adjusted.

My brothers and I have been raised as half savages anyway, running barefoot on the beach, so we just stake off one corner of the yard, at the back near the concrete block fence beyond the overarch of the pomegranate tree, where we go quietly in the moonlight to the place where we keep the shovel so we can bury it.

I keep having a dream that we are all in the car, that our mother is driving. We're driving along the Pacific Coast Highway near our old house, and we round a bend in the road and see my father standing off to the side. He is in darkness, his face half-erased by shadows. It is so dark that I don't recognize him until we pass him by. His face is ash-white and hurt, as if he is disappointed that we aren't stopping for him. It occurs to me that we have failed him, that we are still continually failing him in imperceptible ways. There is, for instance, no place to go put flowers on his grave, which might be a normal thing to do. We don't do any of the normal things. There was no ceremony when he died, because he'd committed suicide and his family was ashamed of him.

The reason for burial is that it helps the dead stay dead, as the dead intended. Without a funeral, none of us can remember from day to day that he has actually died. Geo and our mother especially seem to struggle with the concept. Our mother keeps waking up from her naps on the gold Naugahyde sofa bed and asking us, Isn't your father home yet? Where's your father?

It is his mother—Grandmother Delia—who is particularly ashamed, as it is against the rules of her religion to kill yourself, so a person who commits suicide cannot be buried in consecrated ground. I think it might be argued, though I don't, that a person as tormented as he was is exactly the kind of soul most in need of whatever solace a religion like hers ought to offer.

His mother is ashamed, while everyone else in our family—which is large and old—is embarrassed that he'd got his name plastered all over the front page of the *L.A. Times,* instead of in some small, laudatory article on its realty or business page, the way his own father always did. And that our father left this embarrassing widow and these three motley urchins, all of whom talk like guttersnipes.

And then there is a final humiliation: that since our father is the only son of an only son, we, these guttersnipe-ish orphaned urchins, will actually be the ones to carry on Our Important Family Name, one that is registered with the Holland Society, since Vandenburghs first washed up on these shores in 1644.

Suicide is rude, unmannerly; it is not very *Holland Society,* it is not very 1644. It is shameful and embarrasses everyone, which is why people never know what to say. It is actually impolite to even mention it, as we are told, which is why we begin to mention it all the time.

Suicide. Suicide. Suicide. Suicide. My brothers and I say it constantly. Our saying it makes people uncomfortable, we notice, so we say it more. We are actually told to knock it off, at some point, to stop it, and if we don't, then we are told to go away. We are supposed to either learn to be quiet or else make up a better story, such as the version that is called The Accident. The Accident goes like this. "He'd been taking medication, he got dizzy, and he went to the roof for air." That version is the one preferred by the more genteel of our grandparents' generation, such as our father's great-aunt Bertha Hopkins, who is somehow related to us, but how exactly I'm never interested in enough to remember.

Our mother has other versions that are elaborated over time. They go way back and back, to what's always been wrong with everything, and this has to do with Calvinism and what it says about the human body, which is that we are born in iniquity, which is another word for Vice, which is another word for the LAPD, which has special problems of its own.

Our mother's versions are infinitely various, as if she's making them up as she's going along, and they always have this little piece of discernable truth in them, which is how she tricks you, so you never know which piece of the story to believe and which piece is complete and utter bullshit. She tells these stories in an ulterior way, that lets you feel like she's letting you in on something that must remain our little secret, but this too has a piece of what I'm beginning to identify as irony, which means this is something you both do and do not believe, in equal parts and completely simultaneously.

We're not ever to go by certain versions, however, to go by any story that contains the word *polio,* for instance, or *TB,* as we don't go by that. We also do not go by Dallas, *Texas,* or Houston, *Texas.* And we're never to believe any story that contains any of the crap about how any of the men in our family have *died in the war.* Men in our family, frankly, do not die in *their* crappy war, she says, because it's rare that they even participate in *their* crappy war.

She talks about all wars as if they are the one same thing. Our father, for instance, did not die in their war because he wasn't actually boysie enough for those assholes to let him go anywhere near their crappy army.

Which assholes? Will asks.

The Higher-Up ones, she says. The Higher-Up in the Uppity-Up assholes who take it upon themselves to decide these kinds of things.

Those Shitheels, she says, to be more definitive.

⚉

Now it is Geo who is getting in trouble. He is brought home one day by the scruff of his T-shirt, which is clutched at the back of his throat by the huge fist of a uniformed cop who will let him off this time—next time, juvie for sure. Geo and his friend, this cop says, broke into the house of a neighbor and tore the place apart, dumping food out of the refrigerator, smearing the walls with mustard and ketchup. Will and I can't believe it is our little brother who's done what they say he's done, which was flushing the living goldfish down the toilet, one by one.

No one can understand this, as Geo and his friend didn't steal anything and it was the house of the leader of the Talako Club, who has always been kind to them. Geo is in the second grade. He can't read and he can't write, and no one can any longer remember when he last said more than two or three consecutive words.

Will just keeps punching people. He fails Latin, punches his Latin teacher. I am ordered by my mother not to set *that* in boldface and put it on the first page of my newspaper.[+]

But my mother needn't worry, as I write only the nicey-nice, I write the girlsie, I write that my father was six-foot-three and handsome, that it is his *prestigious* architectural firm that was building Century City, and I brag about it, though this is a project my father referred to as The

---

[+]But I've anyway misunderstood as my brother's Latin teacher is a shapely woman, as I'll find out later, who wears soft, tight sweaters, and my brother, of course, hasn't *hit* her but may have said something odd to her, as all of us (aside from Geo who doesn't talk) are *always* saying the odd or inappropriate thing.

Heat Death of the Universe. I write that my mother is back working for Walt Disney, that when it looks like she is talking to herself, she is actually working on the songs for a musical comedy set in an animated heaven where all dead animals get to go. It is my grandmother's asshole church's version of heaven that says animals are excluded, as—according to church doctrine—animals do not have souls.

I write a story called "Will's Incredible Will," about my big brother's fabulous fastball. I don't mention that he quit Little League the year before. I report on Geo's unusual gifts, his obvious ESP, his specific birdsongs, that he is St. Francis reincarnate, particularly expert on hermit crabs.

⚬⚬⚬

My mother's madness now consists of her getting wildly drunk, of her wearing her bathing suit, wrapped in a sarong, down to the store on the corner of the main street of La Cañada-Flintridge, where she buys more beer and cigarettes, where she'll mention to anyone who will listen that my father died under the *most suspicious circumstances.*

When she is very deeply crazy, she calls it Your Father's Supposed Suicide. When she is more together, she answers the question What does your husband do? by saying, He was an architect but he committed suicide, as if this were one of the world's best jokes. Or she'll say, He was murdered by homosexuals who were angered because he wouldn't leave us and altogether *join up.*

She doesn't believe it anymore, anyway, at least not most of the time. Someone killed him, she now knows—when she is well enough to remember he is dead—and he'd been surrounded by malignant forces.

Becket had wanted him to go to Texas, where they were building Dallas and Houston, but Johnny had refused, so maybe Becket murdered him. Or he was murdered by psychiatrists who were trying out drugs on him—drugs that, she said, made him really, really sick but that he believed kept him going.

Our mother's being insane makes her take the three of us out of school and move us, by taxi, to a hotel in downtown L.A., where she shops for new and glamorous clothes to befit her new status as a wealthy widow, gets us a babysitter from the front desk, then sits smoking in the darkened bar, where she runs a tab and talks to whomsoever is there and will listen.

When she is more crazy, Marilyn Monroe figures even more prominently in the tale of my father's last year, a story that becomes more elaborate over time to include the involvement of both John and Robert Kennedy, and the Mafia, and the heads of the Roman Catholic Church.

My mother also likes to concentrate on who is secretly gay in the LAPD, and wants to know why—if they are not gay—these men are hanging out in the bathrooms of beachside jazz clubs in Manhattan and Hermosa, getting ready to beat on people as innocent as Johnny.

∞

My mother has money from an insurance settlement, much reduced in amount because his death was ruled a suicide. She is flagrant; her money is running out. She needs to get her hands on what she calls Her Estate. Will tries to reason with her: More properly, this is our Grandfather John's estate—he died suddenly while off in Illinois, visiting other Vandenburghs. At the time of his death, he and my father were estranged. This was because my father, in taking his psychiatrists' advice, had stopped speaking to his mother, his father, and even his sister Nan, who was three years younger than he was and was nothing in the family constellation if not blameless.

My mother begins phoning her friends from Cal long-distance to try to get them to help her with Her Estate—the phone bill from our house on Salisbury Court grows higher and higher. She is given one of the first credit cards, which is a Diners Club—her being issued this card makes her believe she is somehow *meant* to go live in another hotel, where our grandparents can't find us.

She, for all her artistic sophistication, is like a primitive person in her relationship with money. Money, she seems to believe, is like a substance that is issued always from somewhere On High and intermittently, like rain. It comes from her parents, or her husband, or her husband's parents, or the insurance company, or else you find out you have this other little inheritance that has been tucked away for you on your mother's grandfather's side, and that these funds are now finally going to be released, but only if you manage to begin to behave yourself. Her mother's family—the Ainsworths—were founders of the town of Orange.

She begins hallucinating voices, and she is actively paranoid about the LAPD. The LAPD, my mother says, is still vitally interested in us, which is why she parks her new car in the garage and then hides it beneath hundreds and hundreds of beer cans.

After our father died and they lost that conduit to what she said was All Our Money, the psychiatrists who had the rent on their fancy offices on the Miracle Mile began, quite naturally, to take gradually less of an interest in us. She tells me they were driving by our house in *sets of threes*, that anyone could see this, that all you had to do was look.

This is when I begin to understand that it will turn out to be fairly important to my psyche to take what my mother says not particularly literally, in that it usually lies near the truth in the way art will, and will often shine with art's particular valence.

The people are at first interested and concerned, then they aren't. Her psychiatrist calls a couple dozen times, then—when my mother hangs up on him over and over again—he abruptly stops.

The ladies from the Welcome Wagon show up on our stoop. They see the mess this house cannot begin to contain and smile hard at us with their plastered-on fake-ish 1950s smiles. They put their basket down amid the beer cans and ashtrays on the kidney-shaped coffee table, and—as our mother begins to tell them about the angels and communists who are listening in on our party line—they smile harder and back out the door.

៣

One morning, Will, Geo, and I line up along the front-room windows to watch through the blinds as our grandfather finally arrives to take us away from our mother. We are going to live at our Aunt Nan's. We're watching, we've been waiting for this, as we've somehow known this would finally happen. My mother will end up spending years and years in the State Hospital at Camarillo. Our grandfather will come to get us and we will end up at Aunt Nan and Uncle Ned's when our mother loses custody. We will never again be allowed to live with her as her minor children.

Our mother is hiding from him behind the pomegranate tree at the back of the lot, but my grandfather doesn't know this and we will not tell on her, so he looks for her in the garage. He raises its door on its hinge, then stands back as a wave of beer cans, the thousands of beer cans she's been hiding there, begins to spill out around his ankles, this bright metallic river of red and silver and gold.

When we see the shock on his face—on everybody's faces—my brothers and I are glad.

We are our parents' children. We are *embarrassing*, we are *like* them, we are like those who arrive at a party where nothing's wrong and set about wrecking everything, unable to help ourselves from telling and retelling this terrible story, to the hilarity of no one but the three of us.

5

Arsenic Hour

JORDAN! MY AUNT SCREAMS. You knock that off! I want you to stop acting like you've been invaded. And you! She whips around to glare at me. You're to stop provoking him with your pronouncements.

My cousin and I stopped fighting when we heard her coming, but we're still breathing hard, sweating. My aunt is smart, at least as smart as I am—she was in medical school when my uncle made her quit to marry him—and there's no real way to hide things from her. My mother calls her the brains of the outfit.

I am fifteen, Jordy's one year younger. My aunt had four children of her own, then got my brothers and me.

Jordy is—I know—her favorite child, just as I'm the one she likes least.

The skin of my aunt's face and neck and arms is deeply tanned year-round because she's a lap swimmer. It's so thoroughly freckled that looking down into her skin, you can see the flecks of color in all the layers. My father, her brother, had skin like that. He's been dead five years.

My own brothers and I haven't been in this family long enough to know what's meant by the things these people say. I'm not sure, for instance, what a *pronouncement* is.

My Aunt Nan and Delia, our San Marino grandmother, address children formally, using their real names—they're trying to appeal to what is civilized in our natures, so my brother Geo is called George Charles. Grandmother Delia likes to say children are the Limbs of Satan. She's usually drunk when she says this; then she and whoever's in the room with her will laugh.

Aunt Nan is furious, but I am madder still. I've just discovered this mute ability, that of watching her, or anyone, longer and harder than they can watch me. I watch her until her eyes glitter and she has to look away. She knows something, I understand, and whatever she knows is purpling the depths of the skin of her neck and face. Under my scrutiny, her tan is turning gaudy.

Aunt Nan's dark hair is sticking up from the way she combs it back to dry after swimming. She has a cowlick at her hairline that makes her bangs pop up—they come up and sway, like a wave on the verge of crashing. My father's hair was dark like hers, but his, like mine, was curly. They were the only dark-haired ones in a family that is mostly blond. My aunt's hair is stick straight, as she says. I can hardly get it to bend around the rollers when she has me set it for her cocktail parties. She's rich but hates for anyone to know this. She's rich but, as my mother says, cheap-cheap-cheap, so she won't waste money on a beauty parlor. Instead, she goes to a regular barber, who whacks it off into this sleek cap.

Jordy and I fight all the time, but this one's bad. My scalp aches from how he yanked me up by my hair. We're the same size but he's suddenly stronger than I am—this is absolutely new, as is his no longer being the one pudgy boy of my aunt's three. He's stronger than I am, but I'm still faster and smarter, and I know more words. I aim these words at him. I choose them carefully.

000

These are performances, my aunt is saying, in which we demonstrate our complete lack of gratitude. It's four-thirty in the afternoon, the time right before dinner when all hell usually breaks loose, the time my aunt and uncle call the Arsenic Hour. We're fighting and Geo and Thomas aren't to be found and my uncle's just phoned to say he's not coming home, that Visiting Firemen are in town so he's taking them to dinner. He's with Lockheed. He's often out with Visiting Firemen or traveling out of town.

These are performances and we need to knock it off immediately, my aunt is saying.

I don't know what she's talking about. Jordy and I fight for a simpler reason: We hate each other.

It's during the Arsenic Hour that my aunt and her friends sit in the shade by the side of one or another's pool with their long, brown, Coppertoned legs stretched out into the still-hot sun of the late afternoon. They smoke and drink their tinkling drinks and talk about their husbands, who are out with Visiting Firemen or traveling out of town. It's the San Fernando Valley in the middle of the sixties, and the kids stay in the water until our eyes are red and squinty, swimming until our lungs ache. My blond hair has turned mint green from the chlorine.

The mothers wear the tennis dresses they drove home in from the club, or after swimming, they wear wraps, like terry-cloth turbans and caftans. They talk about their husbands as *him*, as if they were all married to the same one man.

My aunt, however, doesn't talk about my uncle. This is because she is a devout Episcopalian, as is Grandmother Delia. Religiousness is strange to me—though I am now baptized and confirmed at St. Nicholas Parish, I don't think my aunt's faith has much of anything to do with me. She doesn't gossip but enjoys listening to the husband stories. I lie flat out, my wet front pressed to the hot cement, face to one side. With my arms by my sides, my eyes squinted, they can't tell I'm listening.

Aunt Nan takes a deep drag from her cigarette, makes some low wry comment. She is droll, my mother says. Then her tilted face, in the shade of her hat brim, lights up with the white of her smile. She keeps her face in shadow, smiling as the others laugh.

She's tall, thin, handsome as a model, but she keeps her face bowed over her embroidery. She's working on vestments for the altar guild of St. Nicholas in Encino. My aunt is from the High Church part of my father's family, as my mother says—she and my father weren't Low Church as much as they were No Church Whatsoever. The threads my aunt is using are wound with filaments of real gold and actual silver. My aunt and uncle are too High Church to divorce—our father's mother's family has been in the country since the Moseses landed in Plymouth Colony in 1633, and there has never been a divorce. They're too High Church to kill themselves or to get themselves committed, as my own parents have done.

Still, I'm watching because something is wrong.

Something is wrong, though my aunt and uncle never argue, being too High Church to ever openly disagree. Instead, they'll have drinks and a discussion, the ironic tone of which I can hear through the wall of the living room. This wall has been made so the living room *communicates*—this is the word that's used—with the dining room, which is also the family room, and it's here that we are very rarely allowed to watch TV, though never on a school night. The things in this wall—fireplace, hi-fi, television—all work from either side, the TV being on a track that lets it slide through and swivel around. My aunt designed the wall one of the three or four times she was redoing this house, which is one of her ongoing and seemingly endless projects.

Is she still adding-on? my mother asks. This is one of the times my grandfather has driven us up to see her at Camarillo, where she gets a day pass and comes out with us to a restaurant for lunch. She says *adding-on* and then smiles knowingly at me, as if we both know this is truly aberrant behavior. One of the times my aunt was adding-on, she added a slide-out cupboard in the kitchen that holds nothing aside from the empty drum and rattle of the hung-up lids to pans.

I hear my aunt and uncle, lean over to look through the open fireplace, made of fieldstone. Her head is down; she's smiling hard at her bright embroidery. The silver of the needles leads the shining gold she's jabbing through. Oh, you talk a good fight, she says.

My uncle's done something for which he will not act sorry. He is teasing, playful. My uncle is very good looking. She takes a deep breath, smokes, presses her lips together. He hates her smoking, so she does it ever more defiantly. They met at Pomona College, he made her quit med school, and now she's stuck at home with all these kids. He's just bought a new Mustang convertible, and he's always out now with Visiting Firemen.

He's done something, and try as she might, she can't forgive him though she positions herself each Sunday in her own pew at the front of the church on the dark burgundy leather of the kneeler, her long tan fingers covering the darkness of her tan face, and prays fervently to God for the ability to do so.

〇〇〇

Though lacking in the virtue of forgiveness, my aunt is the most sainted woman in the neighborhood. She's famous for her good works, for her service to the altar guild and for Girls' Friendly Society and for having her own four kids, and for her then taking in her brother's three when *all that* went completely to hell.

She's so good that she at first took our dog, Ziggy—people said it might help my brother Geo adjust. My little brother's in the fourth grade, and he still can't read or write. He's been held back though he's tested as intelligent. We are all three much too intelligent, our Grandmother Delia says, which is at least *hawwwwlf* our problem. Now my brother Geo's getting so big, he doesn't look like he belongs in elementary school.

Aunt Nan got rid of Ziggy because he fought with my cousins' dalmatian. Murphy's valuable, unlike Ziggy, who was a mutt. Anyway, as my uncle put it, Murphy was here first. Murphy's stupid, which is fine because there's a certain admiration for the dumb in this portion of our family. This is a dog bred for looks, bred without leaving room behind his eyes for brains. Murphy is actually so completely stupid that he once loped, as we all watched, right across the way back of the backyard, behind the swimming pool, and ran right into a spurting Rain Bird. From that he got ten black Frankenstein stitches across his forehead; he looked like someone had finally broken down and paid for a brain transplant.

That's not funny, my aunt says.

Is so, I say back, but quietly, because I'm not allowed to sass her.

Murphy was show quality until he got the stitches. Ziggy was short, black, fattish. They fought because they were both males. Ziggy, like my brothers and I, was poorly disciplined. Aunt Nan took him to the pound, where he was placed in the E Room and *put to sleep*—the E stands for *euthanasia*. Then, to be fair, she had Murphy castrated. Because of med school, she uses the Latinate terms: *euthanized* or *castrated* instead of *altered, fixed, neutered,* or *put to sleep.* Because I'm furious, I say *killed* or *murdered.*

Our dog was killed, then my brother Will was sent to a military academy in San Rafael. One of his roommates is the son of Dear Abby. Another is the son of a prominent psychiatrist and they're both, Will says, at least as screwed up as we are.

Or maybe worse, Will says. He tells me stuff like this when he calls from Union Station. He calls at least once a month, when he runs away from the military academy and comes down to L.A. by train. Last time, he just walked away from drills, still wearing his dress uniform. He's so tall now, people on the train believed he was in the regular Army.

Do you remember the time Mom forgot us at that nursery school? he asks this month when he phones. When she was so late coming they had to leave, so they locked us outside the school and left us on the porch, sitting in the rain?

I have no recollection of this event and am imagining it must have happened when I was very little, before Geo was even born. I'm holding my breath. I can't even breathe out any kind of reply.

They could have been arrested, he says. What they did was against the law.

Who? I ask him. *Our mother and our father?* I'm suddenly yelling at him because I'm so startled. The memory of our parents is fragile, like woodsmoke on a windy day—never do Will or I say a word against them. Never, really, do we even think it. Will and I don't speak ill of them, and Geo hardly ever says a word at all.

Not them, my older brother says. The ones who had the nursery school. Put Geo on; let me ask him.

Geo holds the receiver to his ear, staring at the floor. His nose is huge and extravagantly freckled, shiny red where it's peeled and peeled. The nose itself is big, but the nostrils are absolutely tiny. Through these small holes, my brother has the enormous task of first breathing in, then breathing out. Sometimes, when I sneak out of the house at night, I go around to the boys' wing and stand at the window next to my brother's bed. He always sleeps with the light on, so I'm able to watch him. He lies flat on his back without ever moving, breathing noisily in, then noisily out. I am fifteen years old, and I've learned a couple of things. One thing I know?

This is not the sleep of a child.

∭

When Will runs away and comes down to L.A. by train, he spends one night with elegant Grandmother Delia before they put him back on the train going to San Rafael. This grandmother has just left her big house, where she was—as it's said—rattling around, to stay all year in the beach house at Manhattan. We see her every weekend day when we go to the beach from late spring through the fall—it's so my aunt can check on her.

I've stopped belonging to the kind of family I used to have, which was artists, writers, and intellectuals, and have come to live here in this house of surfers.

My big brother's shown me a picture of a bird he says resembles our Grandmother Delia. It's a brightly plumed bird of prey called the harpy eagle. *Cchchcchchhhhh* . . . Will breathes loudly from deep in his throat, imitating her. Lips drawn wide, he's wagging his tongue in the back of his wide-open mouth, just as our grandmother does when she's drunk and comes bumping down the hall of the beach house to tuck us in again.

When we sleep at her house, she stays up late to play the piano. She has a grand piano in her living room at the beach that was moved from her old house—also an upright, also an antique organ you pump with your feet that we're not supposed to mess with.

As she plays, she drinks vermouth from a tall crystal water goblet. I listen to her ice tinkle.

After a while of playing, she starts weeping on the keys. She drinks, plays, weeps, then comes down the long hall in the pitch black night to tuck us in again, though we're already deeply asleep. In this way, breathing her rasping alcoholic breath, she once came to Geo's bed to lean over the place where he was too laboriously sleeping and woke him up, scaring him so much he threw up apple juice and cashews all over her French-laundered sheets.

∞

My aunt and uncle's house sits on almost an acre of land in a tract that was recently walnut groves. They bought it new, then started adding wings to it—the boys' wing was first. My aunt does the design herself. In this way she's copying my father, her older brother, who was an architect.

She copies him just as I copy my brother Will by being a smartass.

I lie in bed at night and try to imagine seeing this house from above, as an architect might, the wings reaching out and away from one another around the patio that sits in front of the lap pool. I can't imagine my father in heaven, spying on the things I do. Will says he killed himself over the ugliness of buildings, over his having to design the same gross thing over and over again all down the Miracle Mile, like Tishman One, Two, Three.

I want to believe our dad died of the ugliness of buildings, but I remember the look on his face one night, the night when the three of us tricked him.

It was winter; we were living at the beach. When my father came in from work, his face felt freezing to the touch of my lips. His homecoming had a ritual aspect to it. How was your day, dear? he'd always ask my mother, to which she'd say sardonically, Oh, ginger peachy keen. By then they both hated almost everything.

How was my day, Daddy? I'd say, at which my parents both laughed.

This night we called out to him: Daddy! Can we get you *anything*? Your paper? Your slippers? Can we bring you *a beer*?

Our father's face, which was gray with cold and weariness, opened like the quick shutter of a working camera. We brought him the *L.A. Mirror*, which was the afternoon paper, and handed him his beer. We watched him drink, then sputter, then gasp and gag, then spit the beer out. He looked at us, hurt, aghast. April Fool's! we yelled, jumping around. We were all clean and bathed and dressed in our pajamas. We'd splurted the can open using the opener called a church key, poured some beer out, and funneled a big handful of salt into it.

Not funny, I think now, sounding like my aunt. *I'm lying in the dark in another one of these other people's houses, and it's years too late to tell him I am so, so sorry.*

𝄌

Our parents were the way they were, Will says, because they were bohemian. The others in our family are all upper middle class, or petite bourgeois, as Will says. He says this the way our parents did, in order to laugh at them: *pet-IT ber-goys*. He calls our aunt's house *ber-goys*, her furnishings *ber-goys*. One main reason he's been sent to the military academy in San Rafael is for him to learn to comport himself.

Our tiny, exquisite grandmother is fluent in Spanish. *Comporté bien*, she tells us when she's asking us to behave ourselves.

Aunt Nan's color scheme is marine: all sea blues, sea greens, and the beige she calls *sand*. Her furniture is teak and modern. With six kids at home, she does all her own housework with help only from a once-a-week cleaning lady and Eunice, who's the laundress. My aunt and Eunice work together to wash the sheets and hang them out in the laundry yard by the side of the garage. Our grandmother has her sheets washed and starched and pressed at the laundry, but my aunt believes in the healthy properties of linens dried in the air and the sun.

She doesn't allow us to eat sugar. She swims a mile of laps every morning, then gets out, dries off, and starts smoking cigarettes. She and my mother and our Grandmother Delia all smoke cigarettes— the women smoke because they went to college, because they think it will keep them from becoming fat. My uncle says smoking is a filthy habit. My aunt says cigarettes are cheaper than tranquilizers. My grandmother owns stock in R. J. Reynolds, so she smokes with small, patriotic puffs.

My aunt swims laps and makes us do so, too. The biggest boys—my cousin Jordy and his big brother Graham—swim competitively, and so will Geo and Thomas soon. Lizzie and I are exempted from swim team by virtue of being girls—the girls' team trains at the swim club at different times, so my aunt can't really get us there.

Girls in this family do other, more home-based, more pioneer-seeming things. My aunt's taught me to sew my own clothes from Simplicity patterns, and we save money by shopping at the Samples and Seconds store in Reseda, where the dresses are already ripped from being tried on by girls too big to fit into them. My aunt takes me to her barber for a haircut. My hair is matted and dirty. I almost never comb it, so it clumps at my neck in tangles and knots. My going around like I don't care what I look like drives my aunt nuts. She says I look *unkempt*, but I know what she really means, which is, You look like your mother, who is—as we well remember—*a mental patient!* In a *locked ward* at Camarillo!

So? I think. So what? So I'm supposed to be *ashamed* of that . . . ?

She saves money on the boys' haircuts by doing them herself with her own clippers. She accomplishes this task on the screened-in porch, where she has them sit on newspaper on the picnic table. Her face becomes small and mean when she concentrates, as if she did become a surgeon.

The boys first laugh at one another, at how—with their hair suddenly short—their freckled noses look bigger and more sunburned and their ears stick out from their scalps. Then it comes to be their turn. Jordy and Lizzie have my aunt's dark hair, while Graham, Thomas, Geo, and I are all blond, so the four of us look more closely related. She leaves each boy with only the slightest fringe in front, which he can comb upward with Dixie Peach Pomade. Everybody laughs at everybody else and somebody always cries.

I'm spared homemade haircuts and swim team and Poopy Patrol, which is the cute name given to picking up after Murphy in the yard, because I am a girl. Lizzie and I never have to do yardwork, as that's what boys do while girls work inside.

And because I'm a girl, I'm prohibited from setting foot in the boys' wing, which is exactly where I go if I ever find myself home alone, something that almost never happens. My aunt designed the wing as one long room divided by built-in bunks and closets, one desk per alcove, one alcove per boy. The ceiling is papered with the eerie see-through blue of sunlight breaking into a thousand pieces in the waves in dozens of surfing posters. I study them as I lie on the top bunk, right next to a closet wall, breathing in and out like my little brother does. I dream of drowning, of being dead, which would be like being extinguished; dream, too, of the weight of various boys I know from school lying on top of me.

My aunt's calling me from the kitchen, but I cannot be found.

She wants me to help look for Lizzie's kitten, which has been gone all day. My aunt calls one more time, then takes the little kids—Geo, Thomas, and Lizzie—out through the laundry yard.

As soon as they're gone, I go into the boys' bathroom to smell their things. They have different products than girls do: powder for athlete's foot, a tube of Clearasil, acid for Graham's plantar warts. Graham's a year ahead of me in school. When we pass in the hall—though we look alike—we ignore each other by tacit agreement. I put his gunked-up safety razor to the side of my own face and watch myself in the mirror. It would be easier on my aunt, I know, if I were not a girl—she knows what to do about boys, at least: drive them here and there, drop them off for sports, ship them off to San Rafael to learn to behave themselves.

I go out to walk through the lines of still-damp sheets in the laundry yard—the smell of bleach and wet and cleanliness is better than any perfume, and I feel it on my face and arms. I climb up onto the half fence, then onto the roof of the bike shed, from which I can boost myself onto the redwood shakes of the garage. I climb the slope to the top of the garage roof, where I can lie on my stomach and peek over while well hidden by the leaves of a huge walnut tree.

I'm watching them: the way my aunt is so sure of what she's doing. This confidence comes, I believe, from her faith in God. I'm watching her shepherding the kids as they go door to door, the little boys taking every other house, my aunt and my cousin Lizzie going up to the ones the little boys are skipping, she having organized them to hopscotch efficiently.

It's Lizzie's face I'm watching. She's eight years old; her face is pure and innocent. Nothing bad has happened to her yet, so she doesn't even know to resent us. According to Jordy's version, when we came it wrecked everything—we remind my uncle of tragedy, so he started staying away. Jordy calls us The Invasion. It's Lizzie's kitten that's missing, but she doesn't think it's dead. Instead this is exciting, it's new, so she looks eager, interested.

෧෧෧

My uncle says I'm his favorite niece, that he's my favorite uncle. This is a joke because I'm his only niece and, since my mother was an only child, he's my only uncle. I'm his only niece because boys run in our family. My uncle wanted a daughter but had to wait through three boys to finally get to her. Lizzie is like my aunt: the baby girl, the youngest. My aunt was my father's favorite person.

Thomas prefers not to be called Tom, or Tommy; he wants his serious and formal name to be used. It's because he's the youngest of my aunt and uncle's boys and he wants to distinguish himself somehow, something my brothers and I will never have to worry about, having been distinguished forever by our parents' actions.

I'm lying on my bed, watching Thomas out my window. He's talking seriously to some grown-ups at my aunt and uncle's cocktail party. He says something to someone not the slightest bit interested, then pushes his glasses back up his nose. He's saying something about how his middle initial is actually NMI, meaning No Middle Initial; that by the time my aunt and uncle got to Thomas, they'd run out of good boys' names.

That's nice, honey, some big-busted, hairsprayed, Hollywood-type woman is saying to my little cousin, as she's reaching past him to get at what she really wants to do, which is pluck some fancy toothpicked food chunk from the ornamental pineapple on the buffet table. Many of the people in our neighborhood are modestly famous because they work in what people here call The Industry.

Thomas! I'm trying to caution my cousin through my powerful powers of mental telepathy: *Movie Lady doesn't give a shit about your No Middle Initial, doesn't care about dinos, either . . .*

This decorated pineapple, also some of its jolly pineapple friends, are all bristling gaily with chunks of orange cheese, big pink shrimp, and cubes of ham, all of which have been stuck into them with bright and frilly cocktail toothpicks. The idea came from a women's magazine. I am one of those responsible for the way these pineapples are now sitting there, completely armored with snacks. While we were doing it together this afternoon, I told my aunt, You know, this is *exactly* the kind of fun-type item—and I showed my aunt a pretty party toothpick—that makes me want to kill myself.

That's not funny, Jane, she said.

Is so, I said back, but quietly, at which she fluttered her eyelashes involuntarily, which meant she was furious with me.

No, *really,* I went on, at least seven Americans die annually of tooth-pick death. I added, Goes in, gets swallowed, gets lodged sideways.

They do not, she told me.

Do so, I said. And they die from choking on party balloons, which is completely easy to understand, the way little kids will get a balloon and put it in their mouth and bite it until it pops, and a piece of rubber snaps back into their throats and completely seals their airways.

Where do you get all this? my aunt asked.

I shrugged. Here and there, I said.

Why do you imagine we need to know these things?

Be prepared? I asked. Or maybe it's only depression, I add, which is really truly epidemic in our family, do you realize this?

What I do about depression, my aunt said, is either swim or pray, or if that doesn't work, I do both.

I was thinking, *You!* Even *you* are depressed sometimes? But I didn't ask her this. Instead I went on saying what I was saying, which I was saying in order to be what one of my grandmothers calls Negative and the other calls always being *anti*-this and *anti*-that. I like to concentrate on the grim details, on the way kids die every day from aspirated balloons or choke on a chunk of sucked-down hotdog that really effectively plugs the airways, or of accidental woundings from a lead pencil, which is poison, which is why they're switching to graphite, or from flukeily falling out a window or having a tree fall over on you or getting hit by a car as you cross the street in the crosswalk, completely minding your own business.

※

It's later that same night. I'm in my room with the light out, looking back into the lit-up portion of the house, where her party is going on. I can't see my uncle, which means he's probably in the family room. I'm no longer talking to my aunt and I'm no longer helping.

Before the screened porch was added, my windows opened to the outside of the house. It's hot—the sliding glass doors to the living room and dining room are all standing open so air and guests can circulate, and my own windows are open so I can overhear.

Lizzie's kitten, which I've been keeping in the record cabinet of my mother's hi-fi, is meowing. I go and get it out. There are clots of shit in there on my mother's albums. My mother loves musical comedy but I don't, but I keep her albums anyway, not to listen to but to gaze at as I remember her. She has *South Pacific, Oklahoma!, Annie Get Your Gun,* and *My Fair Lady.*

The kitten's fluffy and purring. It weighs so little that my hand holding it feels only the slightest heft, a tiny piece of fur and its vibration. I cradle this purring bit of pale gray fluff to hold it to my face, but then, as I feel myself beginning to love it, this gets in the way of what I feel for my own things, my own mother and father, my own brothers, and especially Ziggy, who was my own dog. I miss my mother, so I open the top of the console, where the record changer is, and breathe in deeply the air that stays in there because I never leave it open. By keeping the lid down all the time, I'm saving the air she breathed and that still belongs to her, as it contains her smell.

I open the door to the hall and push the kitten out. It moves off on a diagonal. I close the door and go back to my window.

My aunt's wearing a sleek, black, beaded evening dress with spaghetti straps. Her back is tan and lean. She has a red flower in her hair because of this party's hula theme. Her dress is one that has arrived unbidden, sent by Grandmother Delia, who bought it for her at some chic, expensive shop on Wilshire Boulevard in Beverly Hills. Our grandmother likes to shop by phone, to arrange to have a package brought round by messenger, using the unexpected delivery as a form of wordless criticism. She's recently had a vanity table and chair delivered to me. I sometimes look at them, about the least likely objects I would ever own. *Exquisite*, I can hear her saying as she ordered the fancy mirror, the delicate wrought-iron legs that hold the glass tabletop, the sweet chair that's covered with the most darling pink plush fur.

The card that came with the furniture wasn't signed. It read: "Stand up straight and get your clothes on right."

I look at the card over and over and think, *What the hell?*

The three shiny bumps on top of my aunt's head show the crimp of the roller pins where I put her hair up for this party—she makes me do it, though I totally lack hair skills, just as she does. She doesn't believe I can't do it, because, like my mother, I am artistic, and my mother, very famously, could cut hair. My aunt thinks I can make her hair look good and even stylish if only I put my mind to it, when this is completely outside the realm of any possibility. Besides, she doesn't take time to pamper herself.

Father Robert Gerhardt of St. Nicholas Parish is one of my aunt and uncle's party guests. My aunt looks young and shy around him, like she knows Father Gerhardt is watching. We call him Father Bob. Because we're Episcopalians, our priests can marry and have families, but Father Bob isn't married and lives in the rectory with his mother, who is English.

Because he's a priest and is dressed in black with his white collar, he makes people nervous. I watch them talking to him for a moment, smiling too warmly, then moving away so they can snarl and swear and think bad things. He is actually a pretty cool guy who talks to us in youth group on Sunday evenings about our fucked-up families.

He is sitting on a dark green and blue plaid chair that goes with the theme of sea and sky and hula-ness.

You know, I told my aunt as we were pinning the crap on the pineapples, even the sound of the word *Hawaii* somehow makes me want to kill myself. That was when she told me to go to my room and not come out, saying *that* would be about enough of *that*.

Father Gerhardt is holding his drink in one hand and has a toothpicked shrimp on a fancy napkin balanced on his knee; this shrimp is covered by his tented fingers. My cousin Thomas is bothering him— Thomas and Geo are both in training to be acolytes, so Thomas is trying to get him to pay attention by talking to him about a thousand thousand years ago when the dinosaurs roamed the earth.

Father Gerhardt is also listening to an angry lady who's still mad at him for when he spoke from the pulpit in favor of the Rumford Fair

Housing Act. We are all in favor of desegregation in our family, of de-segregating schools and neighborhoods and workplaces. We're in favor of desegregation since it in no way affects us, since no one in our family has ever known someone who was anything but completely white, except the help, and except when traveling to far-off countries. When Father Gerhardt spoke in favor of Rumford Fair Housing, more than half of the congregation got up and walked out.

Now he's keeping his shrimp resting on his knee because the lady's too angry to have a priest eat food in front of her, and he doesn't want to mix up the mess of eating with what he's supposed to be doing as a priest, which is listening carefully.

He's paying patient and courteous attention to what she's saying, even as his eyes track my aunt as she moves around the room. He puts his drink down, swipes his palm down the length of one thigh, and puts the shrimp down on the side table on top of its napkin, where it will stay, uneaten. He's a man, I see, who's virtually overwhelmed by what it takes to be at a party, and he looks over at my aunt longingly, as if he is there only because of her and only she can save him. Then he crosses his leg the wide way, to show he's not a fairy, and this is exactly when Lizzie comes into the living room to show her mom the kitten and all happy hell breaks loose.

I've just learned that in the San Fernando Valley at this hula-themed party, a screened-in porch goes by the name *lanai*.

◌◌◌

I'm lying flat out on the shake roof of the garage, hidden by the bending branches of the heavily laden black walnut tree, whose nuts hang in their bright green sheaths like an odd kind of fruit, slightly smaller than tennis balls and good for walnut wars.

I can hear Jordy climbing up the bike shed behind me—he's no doubt mad at me over something I said or did and I can't even remember any longer.

I'm eating a bag of Corn Nuts while I watch for Father Gerhardt's Karmann Ghia, which will pull onto our street and drive two blocks north before it pulls into our driveway. He comes to visit at least once a week, always during Arsenic Hour. If it's four-ish, he and my aunt have tea; if it's more like five, they have drinks my aunt makes at the two-way bar.

Corn Nuts give you horse breath, my cousin has, evidently, climbed all the way up here to tell me.

Oh, go to hell, I say, but mildly. He's as annoying as a constantly droning insect, so I'm trying a new tactic, which is ignoring him. I'm watching my aunt as she suddenly opens the front door and looks out, imagining the entry as a guest might see it: bright flowers on either side of the door in blue enamel pots her mother brought her from Mexico. The entry's new, added on in the last round of addings-on, when the master suite was built out into the front yard.

The floor of the entry is greenish-black polished slate and hard to maintain, so she works away at it. Her perfume, a fragrance called Replique, seems to pool right there at knee height when she's subtly dressed up for Father Gerhardt's visit and can't keep herself from buffing.

You can't swear at me, my cousin says. This isn't your house. You don't even live here.

Oh, go to fucking hell, I say. I sound bored, unimpressed by the way stupid fucking Jordy is now standing over me and straddling my body. He is upright on the shakes, which are slippery with moss and lichen, so he's holding on to one of the larger branches of the walnut tree. He's wearing moccasins but no socks, and there are calcified knots on the tops of his feet from kneeling on his surfboard. The skin along the top of his feet and as far up his ankles as I can see is deeply brown and as hairless as a girl's. He has hair now in other places, which I know because he's been moved to Lizzie's and my wing and we now have to share our bathroom with him, where I find evidence of his recent puberty.

With one set of toes gripping through the mocs, he lifts the other foot and takes a little kick at my side. I said, he says, you *may not* swear at me.

Oh, up yours, I say. Up yours, actually, with a ten-foot pole. I'm watching Father Gerhardt's little burnt-orange sports car turn onto our street and start toward our driveway. He drives carefully, like a priest, with his hands on the steering wheel at ten and two o'clock. I am watching him so intently that it's a surprise that Jordy has started huffing, kicking his lame little ineffectual, one-footed kicks at me.

Know what, Jordy? I ask him. You kick like a fucking girl.

Which is when he actually goes a little bit nuts. He falls on me right there on the roof of the garage and is sitting on my hips and weeping down upon my shirt as he slugs me. I turn to look at him.

Jordy's eyes don't match—he has a brown one and a pale green one that's more or less the color of the sheathed walnuts. His eyes put me in mind of the word *diabolic*, and of how our grandmother always uses a foreign language to correct us, saying, *¡Callaté!* to us in Spanish.

Your mother's *crazy*, Jordy's saying, even as he weeps down on me. You don't even *live here* and you can't even *say* the stuff you say. Your father threw himself off a roof, just like you're going to do. He starts prying at my fingers, trying to get me to loosen my grasp.

Jordy is one of Father Gerhardt's favorites—he serves as an acolyte behind the rail, helping with communion. He's at church all the time for this or that and is easily the most devout of my aunt's children. Still, he doesn't want to grow up and have a peaceful profession. Instead, he says, he wants to be a sheriff, though this is the kind of wish most boys outgrow by the time they're six. Everyone knows it's so Jordy can enforce the rules. Jordy is, has always been, rulebound, and very interested in everybody else's going by the rules as well, though the rules, in the part of the family I come from, aren't anything about which anyone really gives a shit.

Well, I say imperiously, in my best imitation of Grandmother Delia, my mother *may indeed be* crazy, and my father *may have* committed suicide, but at least *they* didn't have *a thing* for the parish priest.

I'm lying on my stomach and cannot fight back. He smashes his fist into the center of my back as hard as he can. He's saying things that even he can't really understand, as he tries to pry my fingers up. Then he abruptly stops, stands up, and slides back down the slope on the slick soles of his mocs—the shakes are mossy and stained with the rounded shapes of exploding walnut husks that pelt down in wind or rain.

He hops off the bike shed, then runs across the side yard by the boys' wing with Murphy rocking along next to him. Murphy's so stupid he thinks Jordy's romping alongside him, that they're both having a little impromptu fun, though my cousin has his fists clenched tightly at his sides and is sobbing so loudly I can still hear him.

Jordan! my aunt calls from the back of the house. What in God's name is going on?

Nothing! he shouts out angrily, but my aunt knows, I know, because my aunt knows everything.

I'm silent, dry-eyed, still holding my bag of Corn Nuts. He's weeping from frustration, I understand, that I'm nothing but a girl who doesn't even live here and he still can't make me cry. He doesn't get it; he thinks he has this strange cousin who never cries, when what I really am is someone who once did cry, then suddenly didn't.

✹

It's because Jordy's been so mean to Geo and Thomas in trying to get them to behave that he's been moved from the boys' wing to the oldest part of the house, which is the hallway along which Lizzie's and my bedrooms are. This is why we three all need to share a bathroom now.

Every night Jordy waits behind his closed door to hear when I start down the darkness of the carpeted hallway, always being as quiet as I possibly can. Every night I almost get there, but his bedroom is at the corner right next to the bathroom and across from it, so all he needs to do is open his door, take two steps, go in, and shut the bathroom door behind him, which is what he does every night after he listens patiently to hear me coming.

It's been going on now for days, for weeks. Jordy never gets tired of doing it—I can tell it's what he's thinking about when he looks at me at dinner and smiles his triumphant, weird-eyed I-was-here-first smile.

Graham and I usually have almost nothing to do with each other but recently have started speaking really softly to each other about Jordy. We speak of him in the third person because it bothers him.

Left-handed, Graham says. It's the origin of *gauche*, also *sinister*. They used to burn them as witches.

What do you imagine someone like that would put on his driver's license in the place for eye color? I ask. Answer D: all of the above?

And there's a breed of dog like that, Graham tells me quietly, as my aunt gets up from the table to go get something.

Jordy sits right across from us, on the left-handed side of the dining table. My family is almost all boys, and more than half, counting Will, are left-handed, which is statistically anomalous. The left-handed kids— Lizzie, Jordan, Thomas—all sit opposite Graham, Geo, and me, who are right-handed, blond, and currently looking angelic.

Jordy, I notice, is trying to ignore the new alliance between Graham and me. He's gazing off into later that same evening, when, he imagines, he'll experience yet another bathtime victory.

He always wins and he doesn't get tired of doing this, though it's boring and repetitive and I've begun to notice he's not as quick out his door as he once was, which means he's overconfident and getting a little bit lazy.

I never win; then one night, I do. I'm wearing the shoes Graham and Jordy tease me about—these are dark brown clunky oxfords. I wear these shoes on purpose, even though dressing like this is a chop. I wear them though Jordan and Graham call them my Little Man Shoes. I wear them because they remind me of my father. My father wore dress shoes made in Italy. He had them professionally shined.

This night, the night I win, I am wearing my leather shoes, nothing a normal girl would wear, and I get one foot into the doorjamb before my cousin can manage to lock it.

We're whispering hard words at each other through the crack in the door so my aunt won't hear us. She's off in her wing of the house, sewing vestments and listening to *La Bohème* as she bends over her embroidery. She goes off by herself to listen to opera because my uncle can't really stand it. He calls it *caterwauling* and plays his own music loudly in the living room. His favorite singer right then is Nancy Sinatra; his favorite song of hers is "These Boots Are Made for Walking."

My turn, Jordy guy, I tell him. My voice is sweet and persuasive. Fair's fair, I say. I'm taking my turn tonight, Jordy-Pordy-Lordy. I'm going first this time.

No you aren't, Nikita, he says from the other side of the door he's trying to close. You don't even live here, Fidel.

If I don't live here, I ask, why do I keep turning up like this, day after day after day?

Jordy thinks my parents are communists because they were the first people in our family to stop voting Republican.

You kick like a girl, I say. Know that, Jordy. Plus, you're weak willed. You're just a stupid surfer acolyte and you cry and cry. You didn't think that you, in the whole huge scheme of things, were actually going to win, did you?

I am more determined—this is what I have, it's my secret, it is what will always save me, I can wait and wait. I can outwait him, I can outwait anyone. I sense him inside wavering. I use this wavering in his resolve to shove the door back so it rides up over his toes. He yelps and starts hopping around on one foot, like he's severely wounded, which he quite frankly is not. He's doing all this silently, so my aunt won't hear him. Fighting is now completely prohibited since we got in trouble last time. The next time we're caught fighting, Jordy and I will both be grounded for most of the rest of our lives.

I walk in calmly, lean over, turn on my bathwater. I am acting like he's invisible. He's still hopping; leftover tears still fly off inadvertently from his mismatched eyes. His face is so twisted with pain of various kinds, I practically feel sorry for him.

Get out, I say, or I'm telling her you busted in here while I had my clothes off in order to spy on me, and in saying this into the air, I make it real and so begin to unbutton my shirt, which begins to show my bra, which is when Jordan begins to understand the many and profound ways in which he has so totally and forever lost this war, the wrong one, the one he never knew he was fighting.

But he doesn't want to give it up, which is how we all are when it's our childhood and we're suddenly so terrified of losing the only thing we've ever known. So he comes flying like it's still before, back in the Olden Days, and we fall to the floor and are wrestling around in the same old way, though the charge of it is completely different, and my aunt, who has always known everything, is suddenly there at the door, pounding on it with the flat of her hand and yelling.

We freeze. We watch each other's faces, we are intent on the frozen look on the other one's face. Jordan, she says, turn the water off! Leave some hot water for others.

All right, my cousin says. He and I stare at one another and his eyes have suddenly opened and he is startled by what he's thinking. It's as if we've just stumbled into this strange new place, like the pioneers did when they walked west across the entire country and crossed into a desert of Deep Geologic Time that had landforms in it that were simply beyond their understanding.

My cousin is afraid, but this is because he's a boy and he is younger than I am and he hasn't lived through all I've lived through, which has made me eerily confident. I am confident and determined to make myself at home in this new place and he senses this in me so now he'll mind me, I know, no matter what I tell him to do.

Turn the water off, I mouth. I am moving my lips, making no sound at all.

Water off, I tell him. *Then go, and lock the door.*

6

Some Boy

I AM TURNING SIXTEEN, and I'm being raised by relatives, which means I have to learn to adapt to the rules of what feels like a different country. I try, therefore, to assimilate, all the while keeping my most true self— this is the child who is my own mother's daughter and my own father's daughter—hidden away from them. I am as odd, as strange as my parents were but I am better at hiding it. What I am hiding is myself, and it's like I've shoplifted something valuable that does in fact belong to me, but I have to keep it safely out of sight, grasped in the palm of my hand that I then keep shoved deep into the front pocket of my jeans.

My aunt says I'm not to slouch. She says it; I glare at her. I'm as tough as the boys but I can't win physical fights with them so now I have to boss and trick them. I must become better at being a girl, an identity that's vague to me, inexact, and hard to fathom.

My cousins and my little brother keep reptiles and amphibians: salamanders, snakes, also a chameleon that changes colors not only in different surroundings but also according to its moods. I'm like this— learning to dress in a new bright way, a chameleon turning all her happiest colors. I am tan. My hair is now long and blonde and straight. I live in a household full of surfers so I've become a surfer. Jordy and I have become friends. He minds me and we share effortlessly, as if we're brother and sister. We have a board we have to share with the littler kids, which is a Hobie and wrecked, both dinged and waterlogged, but I don't care because I don't really care about surfing. The board is long and old fashioned and heavy. It's so ugly it's a chop, but I only own my part in it so I'll be asked along by Graham when he and his friends head out early, even before dawn, so early the day comes alive in the east with the morning light as we drive north toward Trestles or south toward Orange County, where we surf Doheny Point or Rincon. I go with them so I get to be with boys.

Graham is an amazing surfer and is turning out to be a friend of mine. The girls sit on towels and sunbathe and talk. At home we put lemon juice on our hair to bleach streaks into it as we lie out by the pool, then we set it and iron it straight and go to the beach, and we don't swim because getting wet would wreck all the work we've just put into it. All the boys surf except for Robert Burlingham, who's thuggish and hangs around us like a shadow. Robert's a friend of Graham's, not mine.

Robert's the oldest of the Burlinghams—his parents, Sarah and Michael, are from England and are close friends of my aunt and uncle's. Together they play bridge, go out to dinner, drink. The mothers sometimes take all the kids on joint camping trips.

Robert's the oldest of four children: three boys, then a girl. The youngest is Katrina, who's the same age as my cousin Lizzie. Robert is Graham's age or maybe older, but he's been held back, so sometimes we have classes together.

Robert's the only one of the Burlingham boys who's dumb. Not only is he dumb, he also isn't that good-looking, as his face comes forward hawkishly and his forehead looks Neanderthal—my eyes see and my mind notes this, while my body has meanwhile begun to pay attention to his.

I see what Robert Burlingham looks like, I note that he isn't that good looking, but what my mind knows my body doesn't seem to care about, as it's my body that reacts to him, so it becomes alert and even nervous when he's around.

Now it's complicated: If my body decides it likes the body or maybe the look of the lips or the neck of a boy, it moves through the house toward the boys' wing where this boy might be. Robert Burlingham is sometimes over, visiting my cousin. But my mind and mouth disparage him, insulting his bad grades in algebra, and Robert, who doesn't like me either, insults me back, saying my being a freshman of the most lowly sort—this is called being a B-9 to his A-9—is the biggest chop of all. It's a symptom of how dumb he is that all Robert can come up with is to criticize my being a half grade behind him.

And no one would ever accuse Robert Burlingham of being clever, but my body is oblivious to his stupidity. He does have command in the social world and wears a letterman's sweater for swim team, as does Graham.

Michael and Sarah are wry and sophisticated. Michael went to boarding school in Austria and skied with my father, and he's somehow related to Louis Comfort Tiffany, as people often mention, and I'll nod though I have no idea who this is.

So Robert is anyway always around, hanging out with Graham, watching TV in the boys' wing, and he's someone I run into not only in the halls at school but in the kitchen of my own house, in which case he and I each make faces and say, *Ewww, gross.* Robert doesn't like me any more than I like him but his body is aware of mine, too, so when his real girlfriend breaks up with him, he asks me out.

We're supposed to be going to some event—maybe this is a dance that's sponsored by a church or maybe it's Cotillion—but instead we go to the drive-in, where we make out throughout the entire movie called *Soldier in the Rain,* starring Steve McQueen. This is the first time I understand what sex is and why a person might get caught up in it, even though you don't basically even very much like this boy or very much respect him, in that your body doesn't actually care that he isn't as smart as you are and he isn't even consistently nice to you, sometimes saying hello in the halls, other times ignoring you because he's walking along surrounded by all these bitchen girls from his own grade.

It's that you like the way he smells and the way his mouth tastes and that the soft insistence of his tongue seems like exactly the right kind of tongue to you and his lips are shaped just so and have a softness and a firmness, but it is honestly mostly his weight on you, the actual physical weight of this boy lying on top of you in the back seat of his mom's station wagon, as he's trying to shove your shirt up to get at what you know he calls your tits, though you won't let him because he's basically a clod who isn't even your boyfriend, so you shove his hand away whenever he moves it toward you, and you'd probably let him feel you up if it were not for the fact that your underclothes are, as usual, wrecked, what your grandmother calls *disgraceful*, in that they're all old and you refuse to sew your bra back together so it's just this ruined thing held together with safety pins.

My aunt and his mother belong to the daytime bridge club in the neighborhood, and our families vacation together in San Clemente during the month of August, where my aunt and Sarah Burlingham rent side-by-side houses to hold their ten kids and all these dogs and even grandparents. Grandmother Delia, who hates being left out of anything, comes along—though she's a redhead and won't go in the sun, so she stays in the house away from the beach, cooking magnificent French

meals with dainty vegetables she gets at Jurgenson's, like white aspara-
gus that comes in cans, and meat whose sauce so reeks of wine that
us kids won't eat it—and there's Robert all the time, looking at me
cross-eyed or sourly or in a smartass way, with him and Graham talking loudly about which girls they *really* like, which has to do with their
having tits or not.

It's nothing but boys at the beach in August. Because Lizzie and
Katrina, who's called Missie, are so much younger than I am, I sometimes hang out with Jordy. My cousin and I barely even remember how
much we hated each other when I first came to live there; now he and I
are the closest friends.

"Familiarity breeds contempt" was one of our Grandfather
Vandenburgh's sayings, or so my mother tells me (I can hardly remember him), but Jordy and I are like an old married couple who have mutual interests. We talk, bodysurf, fish, watch the same TV shows, have a
shell-and-rock collection. We beat each other at chess and cribbage, at
which we're pretty evenly matched.

But at the beach one late afternoon during those last sad days of
summer, when the shadows in the sand elongate and suddenly become
so dark they look like holes that drill down into the middle of the earth,
and the light changes in such a dramatic way it's as if it's meant to il-
luminate everything's emptiness, Robert Burlingham lets it slip that he
and I, in those days of yore, didn't go to Cotillion and ended up instead
at the drive-in movie, not watching *Soldier in the Rain*. Everyone stops
what they're doing—eating mixed nuts, reading comic books, doing
crosswords, or playing the game of War—and turns to stare at me.

I am usually in hiding in this family, which is like a foreign country,
in which I try to dress as much like a boy as I can and come and go as
if I were a boy, so everyone turns to look at me, as if I've been an im-
poster or a spy and am suddenly being revealed as the girl I am. Now

everyone's eyes seem to see me differently, as if I'm new to them and they now see that I'm dangerous.

My face becomes instantly hot and it makes no difference that I deny it, saying, In your dreams, Burlingham; my aunt knows it's true in the way my aunt always already knows everything.

So she asks to speak to me privately, and I get up and follow her out of the living room and see Robert Burlingham, the smug idiotic shit, grinning and wagging his too-thick one-brow at me up and down like he's Groucho Marx.

My aunt says that when we get home from the beach I am grounded for the first three weekends of the school year. I say it isn't fair, that Robert's not going to be in any way punished, and she says that's up to Sarah and Michael, and I say but it's his fault, that he's the boy, that he's older than me, that it was his idea, that he only asked me out and took me to the drive-in to make his real girlfriend jealous.

No one, my aunt says, ever said anything about any part of this being fair, and she gestures around at not only the dumpy little vacation house where we've all been stashed away for the entire month of August, but also the entire circumstance of what it is to be the woman my aunt is or my mother is, one who's educated and sophisticated yet finds herself perched here on the very edge of the civilized world, far away from everything she once imagined she might care about.

And of course it isn't fair, I realize, that my aunt—who was once in medical school—is now stuck in a crowded vacation house that smells of wet towels and mold, with dogs and mostly boys, the one saving grace being that at least Sarah Burlingham, who's witty, is along to hate it with her. And there's our drunken Grandmother Delia, as well as assorted female relatives, such as Great Aunt Hoppy, or a loopy cousin of my dad's named Jocelyn, who've been imported to make a fourth for bridge, while the husbands—who come down only on weekends—are back in town, drinking delicious alcoholic beverages while eating out at expensive restaurants with who knows, and making money hand over fist.

Because this was the West, where women grew up knowing it was never fair, that fairness played no part in it. This was ingrained in Our People, as my mother calls girls and women, and it was never Our People who wanted to come west, as their journals make abundantly clear. They believed this place to be their soul's death, that they were doing this out of self-sacrifice, in which they were trained from their earliest moments; that it was for the sake of their husbands and their children and a more prosperous future that they'd leave everything they cherished—hometown, parents, flower garden, friends. Leave everything, even the only landscape their eyes recognized, the cloud shapes that comforted them, weather they might anticipate. There were colors of green that they'd never see again, birdsongs their ears would never again hear.

And no women actively wanted to make the trek, as they were medically at risk and taking their lives in their hands. There was also nothing for them in the West, aside from a preponderance of men to feed and clothe and in all ways nurture, and—if they survived the trek—physical labor to perform in farming or mining their new claim or maybe, if they were lucky, merchanting. The trek took from late April or May, when the spring mud dried enough that the wagon wheels didn't sink, until the first snows of late October, by which time they'd made it through the coast range, if they were lucky.

They walked behind the oxcart into Deep Geologic Time, through mountain passes, over Basin and Range, into a fold-and-thrust terrain so bizarre it was unlike anything they'd even heard described. They forded rivers of mud that snaked back and forth across a broad and otherwise naked plain, and their wagon wheels stuck in quicksand, so they began to unload anything that was extraneous or decorative or girl-like, anything that let them believe they were bringing civilization with them: any book that was not a Bible, all pictures, musical instruments, art.

They departed Freshwater and trudged out into the Forty-Mile Desert, strewn with the carcasses of livestock and the homely items some other woman had cherished. Nearly four hundred thousand people made the trek by the mid-1800s; between twenty and thirty thousand of those pioneers died. The oxcart emigrants, like those in my family's background, were almost always young families. Many of the women were in some stage of pregnancy or had just given birth, and they bled and were anemic and medically at risk, and their babies died in infancy or under the wheels of the oxcart. They came unaccompanied by their sisters and had no one else to help them with the arduousness of this very terrible life, so some of them came west wearing wedding dresses they'd dyed black to symbolize that even if they made it to Oregon or California, they knew they'd never see their own mothers again, so their lives were essentially over.

And once there, they had to acclimate to what life would have been in the Middle Ages, to live in villages that lacked schools, streetlights, sidewalks, libraries. They'd look forward the whole trek to a place called Nevada City or Oregon City, but, arriving there, would find only a tiny settlement made up of the homesteads of a few families.

Emigrants wrote home words such as these: *I wish California had sunk into the ocean before I had heard of it.*

෴

The only reason I was ever even allowed to go out with Robert Burlingham in the first place was that my aunt and uncle *know him*, know his parents, know that he—with all that Louis Comfort Tiffany whoever-he-was stuff—is from a good family.

This is a strict rule of my dating life: Any boy who invites me out on the weekend must, by Wednesday, have made arrangements to come to my house to be introduced to my aunt, which means this boy's having to sit stiffly upright, trying to think of something to say to my aunt in her sand-sea-and-sky-colored living room, as she smokes cigarettes and fastens her eagle eye on him. This is her most direct and confrontational stare, which seems to say, I have *boys*, I know what *boys* are, I know *exactly* what boys like you are up to.

And I find that almost no boy is interested enough in me to actually show up to this introductory meeting, as my aunt is actually notorious for being strict and even severe. She'll become perfectly silent, which makes you think she can literally read your mind, in which case you're pretty sure you're about to be arrested.

So I have mostly avoided dating, which is fine with me because I basically hate being in a car alone with some boy I barely know, which is awkward, which usually involves my babbling on in a cute fake way, talking all excitedly with my hands, and going out to someplace I have no actual interest in being.

Instead of dating, I go out with Reggie and Steve, who are football players and friends of mine, nice boys—even my aunt likes them. Steve, who is regular, is the quarterback and Reggie, who is Mexican, and a wide receiver. My aunt knows Reggie and Steve because they hang out at our house. We drive around in Steve's red truck to parties or dances, where we go as friends, as each of the three of us is always interested in people who aren't interested in us, which somehow suits us perfectly.

But my being away all of August, then being grounded for the parties at the beginning of the school year, is a complete stone drag, as this is when all the intricacies of the year's friendships and romances are being laid down along a complex social grid of nuance and association. We get new clothes for the start of school, then come as versions of new people, better and more exact copies of the people we're hoping to become. I am adept at *becoming.*

I've always loved September. The school year starts and every class is potentially interesting and my notebook is still neatly organized behind its dividers by subject and I haven't yet messed up and it's a good time to see who's changed over the summer and so become less what they were, which is always because we're teenagers, somehow moist, inexact, and larval—and more the clean dry upstanding people we hope to one day be when we go out to own the world.

But all this is going on without me, which wouldn't have bothered me before I'd lived in my aunt and uncle's house long enough to became better adjusted. To become better adjusted, I've had to very willfully abandon certain allegiances I've had toward my mother—who (and usually for good reason) hates almost everyone and everything, the why of which she can also always perfectly articulate—and become more like my father, who had friends because he, like my aunt, was both attractive and vivacious. Inside the house, I'm still known for who I am, which is my parents' daughter, which means I'm dark and somehow twisted. Outside the house I'm this other more radiant being. My hair's long and blonde and straight. My skin's okay. I'm funny and I have friends.

Besides, I have Graham and Jordy, who arrive at school with me, and my aunt's bought us our own car, even if only Graham has his license, even if it's only this shitty little Renault, the ownership of which is actually a chop. My aunt got it for us so she won't have to lend us her car, the reasons for her not wanting us to borrow it becoming immediately obvious.

So my boy cousins and I arrive at school like this completely bitchen phalanx, a self-possessed cadre of good-lookingness and popularity. And we're suddenly all friends of one another's and our friends are friends of theirs and our friends are suddenly everything to us, as it's a relief to escape finally from who we are within the messy network of our okay-on-the-surface but secretly really messed-up family.

〇〇〇

It's the second weekend of my grounding when Reggie and Steve stop by on a Friday afternoon to tell me there's a party that night. They've come to ask Aunt Nan if I can't go out with them. They tell her they'll keep track of me, and she's charmed by them because they're brotherly and kind and they stand up straight and look her in the eye, like they're not ashamed of what they've just been in the bathroom doing.

Reggie and Steve are what she calls Good Kids. This means they know how to show up on time and behave in a mannerly way. They also dress appropriately, wearing what is almost a uniform of chinos, pressed shirts, and their maroon letterman's sweaters with white stripes on the sleeve for each of their sports.

And I can see my aunt being even tempted, as this would give her the night off from watching me, but even as she wavers she remembers she isn't one to change her mind about rules and punishments.

My aunt doesn't believe in being flexible; she can easily imagine—I imagine—based on my parents' example, where *all that* might lead.

And she's still basically this scientist who didn't finish med school because my uncle made her quit but who still believes things to be logical—that is, set out in a certain way. Fish or cut bait, she tells us, then demonstrates by chopping the chunk of air that's balanced on her up-turned palm with the axlike movement of the side of her left hand (doing this left-handedly, of course), saying, *Bomp, bomp, bomp.* Everything as it is and ever shall be, my aunt believes, as is droned each Sunday in church, world without end, amen, and so on and so forth.

She calls the imagined order of the world its Thus And So.

Steve and Reggie are so well known to my aunt that they're invited to stop calling her Mrs. Snowden and call her Aunt Nan instead, but they're too shy to call a person as formidable as my aunt much of anything. Charmed by them, she wavers but doesn't change her mind, because it has no doubt occurred to her that, aside from the episode with Robert Burlingham at the drive-in movie, there's just *so much* other stuff I've done to get in trouble: the inappropriate clothes I've shown up in on a Sunday morning just as she, by herself, is trying to get everyone in the car for church, while my uncle, who is an atheist for reasons analogous to mine, is still in bed because he's recently announced he will no longer go to church with us.

And there was the episode of my driving my grandmother's car one weekend when us kids were all staying there, though I don't have a license and haven't actually even taken drivers' training, so I don't know how to drive and was so panicked I shifted from park while flooring it, thereby doing what my cousin Graham calls grinding a pound of gears.

Plus, there's all the other stuff she's more than right about, even if she's only guessing.

Robert Burlingham still hangs around our house but I don't speak to him, since he got me in trouble and he—of course, since life isn't fair—has never been punished in the slightest way. Even the girlfriend he was trying to make jealous when he took me out went back to him immediately.

So Reggie and Steve can't get Aunt Nan to change her mind; then a ton of people come over to hang out before going off to the party, so I go to my room, as I can't actually stand it, since I will not be going, and one of these friends is, of course, Robert Burlingham, that shit fuck asshole, whom I still secretly like.

And I'll try to get the stories of what went on out of Reggie and Steve and my boy cousins, although they are all such boys that they're mostly looking only at who has, and I am not kidding, *tits* or not, and *tits* is the word they honest-to-god use when they don't know I'm listening.

And I'll ask them if So-and-So was there and they'll be like, Huh? What? I dunno, no really, I actually have *no idea*, and I'm wondering, *How can you have no idea?* And, feeling pressured, Reggie'll say yes and Steve'll say no, and they'll stare at each other in that blank way that reads as *nnnnnnnnnnn* or boy-mind drone—that is to say, *totally* noncommittal.

And it absolutely baffles me that boys, in general, will let such important details go by without their even noticing.

So I'm sulking and miserable and it's later that evening when the phone rings and my cousin Thomas goes and gets it because he likes to answer the phone, which gives him a chance to say, Snowden residence, Thomas speaking, which always makes me want to get up, go over to him, and strike him really hard in the muscle of his upper arm. But then he holds the handset out to me, saying, It's for you, and I silently mouth, *Who is it?* and Thomas says completely loudly so whoever's there can hear, I dunno, some boy.

And we of course have no privacy in our phone calls, as the only phone we're allowed to use is the kitchen phone that hangs right next to the red Naugahyde booth where we all must crowd in to eat a hot breakfast, as my aunt believes in hot breakfast the way she believes in the Nicene Creed, so we shove in there disorganized by our handedness, showing up by who's ready first. My aunt makes the plates all at once and keeps them warm in the oven, so breakfast's this heat-hardened thing that's accompanied by the chaos of left- and right-handed kids all shoving and elbowing.

I go to the phone and hear this voice I don't know saying it's John Philip Hudsmith.

Who? I ask, though I vaguely know this person from some classes we may have sometime had.

John Philip Hudsmith, who somehow knows I'm grounded, says he's going to be in the neighborhood later if I want to sneak out. If I want to sneak out he can wait in his car under the streetlight over on Oak Park, which is the street behind our street; he'll be there by eleven or so, and he'll wait if I want him to take me to the party.

He names friends who are already at this party, which he says he's already been to and is going back to later, and I'm so eager to get there it doesn't actually bother me that, for someone I hardly know, he knows much too much about me. I figure he's a friend of Graham's or Jordy's, that he's been to our house in one of these pre-party crowds of twelve or twenty that congregate in the boys' wing, talking about who has tits or not and getting ready to go out. These gatherings are always impromptu, as Jordy and Graham and I have never been allowed to have a party ourselves, which is fine with us since my aunt's so strict that she would no doubt die if she knew how we act when she is not around to watch us.

҉

It's ten thirty or so and I'm waiting up, watching television in the family room, hoping my aunt will finally go to bed or at least to the front part of the house to work on the vestments she's embroidering for altar guild, but she's still puttering in the kitchen, which means she is basically hiding food. She puts food Geo and Thomas might sneak, like the cookies she buys in bulk in white paper bags at a certain grocery's bakery, really high on the highest shelf, out of everybody's reach.

She puts all the individual bakery sacks in a big Tupperware tub that's supposedly hidden above the actual cupboards, but Thomas, who is small and agile, has perfected this certain silent stealthy crouch whereby—even with my aunt listening to music in the living room—he can get to that part of the big room that is the kitchen/dining/family room unnoticed and hide behind the cooking island, then use the drawers she's designed to glide out silently to climb to the counter, where he stands up and uses a wooden spoon to quietly lift the tub down. We all watch neutrally, uninvolved, so that if he gets caught it's only Thomas who's screwed. Still, we're all completely rooting for him to get away with it, and we watch as he lifts the cookie tub down and sneaks it over so he can share its contents with the rest of us, so we won't tell.

My uncle's out, as usual. She's finally finished unloading the dishwasher that runs at least twice a day, folding the last dishtowel, turning out the lights.

All set? she asks me.

I nod. I'm barely speaking to her, so I don't take my eyes off the TV screen.

Night, she says.

Night, I answer, still not looking at her.

She turns in the doorway. Well, after this, she says, you only have one more weekend. Then you can be out and about and up to your old tricks.

For my aunt, this is an astonishingly fond and friendly thing to say. My ears hear this and my mind takes it in, but I'm so burrowed into my fury, which is the true dark core of who I am, that I'm far beyond caring about this tiny pinprick of loving kindness.

Right, I say, and I turn to look up at her so I can fix her with my coldest stare.

Geo and Thomas and Lizzie are all in bed. Jordy and Graham are gone in the Renault, which is a rickety foreign car we kids would never have. We've been told its name is said *Rey-NO*, but everyone at school calls it a *Run-ALT*. My aunt needs only a single teenaged driver to help her with kid pickup and incidental errands, which is Graham.

Besides, Jordy's not yet old enough to drive and I am in no way trustworthy, as she and I both know, which was confirmed amply in the incident in the liquor store parking lot, when my grinding a pound of our grandmother's Studebaker's gears totaled its transmission, which then cost, as Aunt Nan said, *the earth*.

⬭

My aunt is so concerned about the harm that might come to me and Graham and Jordy now that we're teenagers and driving and going to parties where there may be drinking that she herself has almost entirely stopped going out in the evenings, so she can be here to smell our breath and otherwise monitor our temptation to self-destruct, which— as she and I both know—is intricately woven into the spiral helix of the very DNA of us, about which I've just studied in Anatomy and Physiology.

Our grandmother is, very famously, a drunken driver who will drive her seven grandchildren while, as my mother says, *plotzed, smashed, swacked, plowed, blasted, blitzed,* or *stink-o*. She will do this even arrogantly when some version of the whole troop of us is staying overnight with her. She'll order us all into the Studebaker, even if Graham or Will is there, who'd be better at driving than she is, and she'll set out in the early evening to go drink with her friend Alice Herbert, though it's abundantly clear the moment we arrive that Alice Herbert has no wish whatsoever to entertain this herd of Delia's bored and errant grandchildren, so the women will just knock back a few quick ones before we're sent on our way. We pile back into the Studebaker, which doesn't have seat-belts or even a back on the bench in the second seat—it's more of a fabric drape that lets us crawl into the trunk, where whatever group of us it is huddles, white-faced and scared, as our little grandmother, who's so short she nearly has to look through the steering wheel and is *snockered, ripped, bombed, tanked-up, wasted,* drives us away from wherever Alice Herbert lives and back through El Segundo toward the ocean, into the more and more dense fog we find on the Pacific Coast Highway, all while accelerating and braking at exactly the same time so, the whole way home to Manhattan Beach, the car lurches and shudders and halts.

Our grandmother is a tiny person, the only woman in our family who might be described as delicate. Her hair's done up in a hair-salon chignon and dyed a color called Champagne; her fingernails are always impeccably manicured and painted to match her hair. She has always competed with my mother and my aunt over any man's attention. This is because she grew up being accustomed to being the most beautiful girl in the room.

She's used to being beautiful and the center of everything. She isn't yet used to having become old and a widow and the mother of a dead son—this would be my father—who wasn't even talking to her when he committed suicide. The deaths of her husband and her son took place within a year of each other and have happened recently enough that she's still being forgiven for the way she's not yet adjusting. People still feel sorry for Delia, my mother says, which is why she gets to act the way she does.

But don't be fooled by my mother-in-law, my mother says. Delia doesn't have a grief-stricken bone in her entire body and she's always been *exactly* like that, which is to say, not only a completely hopeless dipso but also totally, narcissistically self-involved. And she's just so plain nasty, my mother adds, that what she felt when your father died was largely embarrassment.

〽

My aunt knows about her mother's driving the car drunk, though we've never told on her, and she knows about Delia's sending me to the liquor store with a note saying I'm authorized to buy her cigarettes, which is when I ground the pound of gears. I had no idea what I thought I was doing getting behind the wheel of the Studebaker—only that she ordered me to do it, as neither Graham nor Will was there.

My grandmother has never had much use for girls, who either are baby darlings and therefore exactly like she is or—like my aunt and me—exist mainly to do her errands.

My aunt knows because her mother will require certain things of us, swear us to secrecy, then call to tell my aunt *herself* to tell her daughter *herself* exactly what we aren't telling her, as if to demonstrate her theory about how children really *are* the Limbs of Satan and utterly disloyal, so my aunt should never trust us.

So my aunt is understandably afraid of being driven around by drunks, since she probably grew up with that. My parents never drove drunk, though each was almost always completely *blotto* or at least *well oiled.* Instead, when they were *soused, pickled, snockered, juiced,* or *trashed,* they'd famously take taxis at unbelievable expense all around the Los Angeles Basin, and this wasn't just for safety's sake but mainly because it was such a *Not* Middle Class thing to do.

Besides, my mother sniffs, taking cabs made us feel like F. Scott and Zelda.

〽

My aunt has ordered Graham and Jordy and me to never drive a car if we've been drinking, to never get into the car with anyone who's been drinking, that we're not to worry that we'll get in trouble, that being in trouble in this case is suspended, that all we need to do is call—even if we're at her mother's house at the beach—and no matter what the circumstances, she'll drop whatever she's doing and come directly there and get us.

This was after Graham got drunk and threw up all over the front seat of the new Rey-No, which then had to be sent to some specialized car-cleaning shop where everything in the dashboard was taken apart, which is what it evidently takes to get the vomit out of a car's heating ducts.

The night of the party I go into my room and put music on, then begin to get clothes out of my closet. As I do this I play records on my hi-fi, which once belonged to my mother. Hers were albums, mine are 45s, which I stack on a thick spool that adapts the record changer. If you leave the arm out, the same record will play over and over, which is what I do with a song like "Duke of Earl," which anyway sounds like it's playing over and over, as it is and ever shall be, burrowing down through the scales of the earth's rock-hard mantle, downward toward the molten flux, or magma, that—as we've just been taught in Geology—exists at the heart of everything.

I build a body in my bed, and this isn't just some clumsy pillow thing—rather, it is positively sculpted, a girl's body on her side with her back to the door, knees drawn up, face turned away. The body is in proportion and has shoulders, hips, and a waist, and the head, which is made of a tiny pink baby pillow I've probably stolen from Lizzie, is wearing a cloth cap that's filled with my own outsize hair rollers.

I turn off my own overhead light in order to witness what I've made. I view it in the light that falls through the doorway: Girl Innocently Sleeping, which is what my aunt will see if she comes to check up on me, as—and I know this to be so—she sometimes does.

I set two final 45s on the hi-fi and move the arm so the equipment will turn off as soon as the second song has finished. I play "To Know, Know, Know Him Is to Love, Love, Love Him" and Roy Orbison's "Pretty Woman," because they're both sweet songs but muscular enough in tone to hide the movement of bodies in the house, and not so loud that they'll bring Aunt Nan from the wing in the front of the house to tell me to turn my music off.

I haven't really dressed for this party, but I have a bag with clothes and shoes I can change into. For what I'm doing I need to be barefoot, as that's how I'm most surefooted.

Most of the windows in the house have screens on them, which are impossible to climb through, but Graham and Jordy and I have figured out the exits. One of my windows opens onto the screened porch, as does the opposite window in the boys' wing, and these have no screens. Going through the screened porch, you are, however, momentarily exposed through the sliding glass doors to whatever's going on in the living room and kitchen, so this works only when that part of the house is dark. Murphy also needs to be stashed somewhere else than his dog bed so he won't try to come along with you.

You need to go through the dog door because the metal door it's in has no key and locks from the inside and is flimsy and the noisiest one to open.

These houses are all big; most of them have swimming pools, and for legal reasons involving some kids maybe drowning in somebody else's pool, all the walls around people's property are of a certain height, and uniform. These walls are built of cinder blocks and capped with a red tile that makes them about six inches wide. They're so tall you can't see into your next-door neighbor's yard.

My cousins and I, as well as many of the neighborhood's our-age kids—of which there are literally dozens—have long used the tops of the concrete walls between houses as a kind of kid expressway that can take you into the backyard of any other house on our block. These huge yards, their bushes and trees and plantings, can feel teeming with kids, so it's never really surprising to look out a back window and see some friend's face motioning for you to open your window so they can tell you something that's happened that they think you need to urgently know.

We don't use the telephone, because every kid knows no parent will tolerate a phone call made after nine o'clock at night.

You get up on top of the wall from the roof of the bike shed. The wall's wide enough that, barefoot, you can practically run along the top of it like it's the balance beam in gym. You are also almost entirely hidden from the sightlines of the houses by the drape of what's left of the walnut grove, whose trees—at least through late summer or early fall— still have leaves on them.

I know Ted and Sylvia will be out, because they're always out, and so will Cheryl, who is just my age but already gorgeous in a grown-up way and so good at clothes and makeup that her mom's taking her over the hill to do modeling. Cheryl's popular with older guys who aren't even still in high school, so she is rarely home. Dougie, who's a year behind Jordy and socially retarded by his still being in junior high, will be there, as a kid his age has nowhere to go.

Dougie and his little buddies like to spy on us when Cheryl has friends for an overnight and we're getting out of our towel-wrapped bathing suits and into our pajamas after a night swim. We know they're watching, so we put on a show of pretending to strip to "Let Me Entertain You."

Ted's a tyrant but Dougie's so good-natured that he can be talked into anything, so I go directly to the DeCinceses' and climb down off the wall into the V of a certain fruit tree we use as our expressway's on- and off-ramp.

Dougie is friendly, interested, neutral. He doesn't even ask why I'm standing there; he just opens the door and lets me walk through to their all-white living room, where I sit on the white couch to put my shoes on before I go on out their front door.

John Philip Hudsmith has the kind of car certain boys always have— a '57 or some other similar year Chevy or Ford—and I can never pay attention long enough to cars to ever memorize the shapes and symbols and so must always read their names, spelling out *F-o-r-d* or *C-h-e-v-r-o-l-e-t*, to know for sure. His car has the usual new paint job and is buffed and waxed, the way this kind of boy's car always is.

He's been waiting under a streetlight on Oak Park with his lights turned off.

He flicks his lights at me.

Hey, I say, as I climb into the front seat.

Hey, he says back. No one else is in the car, which isn't the way we usually travel. It's about eleven thirty and mist is beginning to rise from the wide front lawns, a damp look that even smells of loneliness and always deeply spooks me.

Where to? I ask.

It's up in the hills, in Chatsworth. At that girl's house, the one who looks like you?

Oh, yeah, her, I say. At Brandy Cannon's?

I've been hearing about this girl ever since I was a freshman in high school. Her name is *Brandy Cannon*. A number of people—maybe eight or ten—have told me that she and I not only look alike, but we're both loud and funny and our laughs sound the same.

I've heard about her but have never been that interested in actually meeting *Brandy Cannon*, as this will show me what I remind people of when they look at me, something I don't necessarily want to know.

I also don't really get her name. I wonder why her parents named her Brandy, as no one is yet named this kind of really out-there thing. The name sounds lowlife to me, or like she comes, as I do, from a long line of alcoholics who think being drunk is *just hilarious!* as we do in my family, hence our million humorous words for *lushes, winos, boozehounds,* who've had *tee-minny-martoonies* or are *three sheets to the wind.*

It sounds like she doesn't really *go with* where she lives. In Chatsworth, kids are richer than we are. In Chatsworth, kids have horses.

John Philip Hudsmith, who actually goes by all three names, which is the kind of thing that makes me cringe, is driving west on Nordhoff, past the cornfields that will soon no longer be cornfields and the fruit stands that are now closed but have until recently been selling the last of the summer's fruits and vegetables. His name—or at least his going by it—clues me in to his being some kind of weirdo, as does the manner in which he's driving. He is extremely tense, though we're traveling down a wide avenue crossing largely empty streets and there's really nothing to be all that excited about. Still, I see his jaw clench and unclench; a little bulge first forms, then disappears as he releases.

He is also driving stiffly, with his elbow out the window, his arm resting on the door, so he looks as if he's completely relaxed, though he isn't relaxed at all.

Nice car, I say, as this is the thing you are supposed to say when you're a girl encountering some boy in a car like this, one with a manual transmission and tuck-n-roll interior that's still fragrant with the new-car smell. I say this though I don't actually give a shit about what kind of car a boy drives, and want only for it to get me where I'm going, which is, I always hope, far away from here.

John Philip Hudsmith anyway shrugs off the compliment.

Isn't mine, he says.

No? I ask.

My brother's, he says.

Nice brother, I say, to lend you a car as nice as this.

Not really, he says. He didn't really lend it to me. Then he turns to me and says, I actually more or less took it.

And this is when I smell his breath and realize that John Philip Hudsmith's been drinking and has also been chewing Juicy Fruit gum to try to cover it up. The smell of alcohol and Juicy Fruit or Wrigley's Spearmint is something I'm actually already acquainted with, though I don't yet drink and most of my friends don't yet drink, as we're still only in tenth grade but we all still somehow already know by teenager osmosis all the tricks of drinking: how you can raid your father's liquor cabinet and water the gin to fill it to the line he's marked on the bottle in grease pencil that's supposed to keep his kids from guzzling it.

And John Philip Hudsmith isn't one of the boys who's ever been to our house. Rather, I've seen him standing on the edge of things, listening, as I myself have often carefully listened while I was learning how to hide who I am in the disguise of a more regular girl.

Suddenly I know all about John Philip Hudsmith, who's a loser who's driving *shit-faced, polluted* in the car he's boosted from his brother, and that he likes me, it turns out, because long ago back in the Days of Yore before I became better at being a more normal teenager I was once nice to him.

This is so sad it makes me want to kill myself.

We're meanwhile cruising around in the foothills of Chatsworth driving up and down wide avenues of houses that are not yet built and he has the windows rolled down because he is supposedly listening for the sounds of the party, but there is no party up here because—as anyone can plainly see—these houses haven't yet been finished and are still only poured concrete foundations, with walls framed in, then stood up like the empty skeletons of lives that aren't yet ready to be lived and all this pretense is because John Philip Hudsmith is what in later years will come to be known as *really into me.*

Which I studiously ignore. I ignore him except to complain generally as if I were what I'm currently pretending to be, which is entitled. I tell him my stomach's upset, that I get carsick, that we're going to have to stop driving around in a minute and really find this party or I may be sick all over his brother's new tuck-n-roll.

John Philip Hudsmith is a great example of the type of boy—as I am only just now discovering—who will *always* fall in love with me, the Honors English–type boy who'll go on to college to major in literature and will want to write the Great American Novel without ever learning to write a single Good American Sentence. This boy will turn out to be gay and will want me or someone just like me—it will really make no difference—to save him from homosexuality. Or, if not gay, he'll almost invariably be Other, as my father was, which is to say he'll inevitably be in conflict about his identity.

Which is to say this boy will be sensitive, which I can't stand, since I'm already so sensitive I can't even stand myself, so sensitive that I can't bear to hear the sound of certain pretty common everyday words and phrases without feeling like I need to cover my ears and go *nah-nahhhhh-nahhhh* the whole while these words are being said to avoid the effect on my body of having heard these things said, which feels like a physical assault.

Which is to say John Philip Hudsmith will be nothing like Robert Burlingham, who's a clod but is at least *different* from me, which makes it interesting. Kissing a boy like John Philip Hudsmith, I already know completely, though I have no experience with this, won't be interesting, because people just like you are never interesting. It's too much like kissing Brandy Cannon or someone else who's somehow equally lifeless, being someone already too well known to your body.

I also know that John Philip Hudsmith, who probably will go on, because of his stupid name, to write really crappy plays that are just too honestly awful to even sit through, isn't really yet ballsy enough at fifteen-sixteen-whatever to pull the car over and park in some cul-de-sac of these still-half-built houses that overlook the dimmed-by-vapor lights of the cauldron of rising mist that is the San Fernando Valley in the 1960s. He can't put his arm around me and try to kiss me, which is—I know now—what this drive around town is about, so I keep chattering on about all our many mutual friends, who are actually *my* friends, not his, saying I really am not feeling well and if we can only get to this party, maybe I can get a ride home from Reggie and Steve. John Philip Hudsmith surely knows *Reggie and Steve!* because everybody knows *Reggie and Steve!* as they're football stars, and a football star is all a high school has in the way of famous.

Soon I'm telling John Philip Hudsmith he has to take me home, but he doesn't really want to take me home, though I am actually honestly beginning to feel sick, now that I've become honestly worried that I may end up raped or dead. At the very least my aunt is going to find out about this, in which case she'll kill me.

Up to my old tricks, and this one, I'm guessing, may actually do it. I've always managed to exist right on the margins of being just too *out there*, skirting along barefoot along the top of the wall along the borders of propriety always, right there teetering but managing not to fall off into the place Aunt Nan calls Beyond the Pale.

Boys in our family get shipped off to boarding school. I don't really know what they do with girls, but I am just about to find out.

ʘʘʘ

I get John Philip Hudsmith to drive me to a gas station by telling him
I need to use the bathroom or I will—*and I swear to God!*—throw up
all over his brother's car, and he will—*I swear to God!*—end up having
to take it to this specialty shop in Sepulveda where they get vomit out
of the heating vents, and it's so expensive they have to take the whole
console apart, which costs *the earth.*

So he drives down the hill and back along Nordhoff until we see a
Texaco sitting in a wash of yellow light that looks as if it's been tinted by
disease, and he pulls in and tells me that if I even speak to the gas station
attendant he will drive away, leave me there, go directly to my house, and
do a lawn job, which'll involve his driving his brother's '57-or-whatever
backwards up onto the lawn, where he'll put the handbrake on and step
on the accelerator to turn the wheels, which will then dig huge chunks of
sod up out of the earth and pitch it back against the house.

Right, I say as I get out of the car and slam the door.

The attendant is wiping his hands on an oily rag as he walks from
the office, coming toward the pump. The attendant is young and his
teeth are bad, his face pimpled in the way of those who are new to
California so their parents don't yet know how to plop them in the fresh
air and sunshine and offer them fruits and vegetables.

Guy's bothering me, I tell the attendant. He's weird and he's been
drinking and now he won't take me home. Can I use your phone to call
my aunt?

Then we both turn as we hear the engine and the tires squeal; we
turn to watch John Philip Hudsmith speed up and corner, skidding wildly away, driving as fast as he can but *with his lights off,* as if this is going
to help him disappear.

I think about who I might call to take me driving around to try to find Reggie and Steve, but it's so late no parent will let me speak to their kid on the phone, and everyone will anyway still be out at parties or else over on Reseda Boulevard at Big Bob's, which is what we call that particular Bob's Big Boy—as opposed to Little Bob's, which is somewhere else.

But I actually already feel so tired and so completely caught, I call my aunt and tell her the short version of what has happened and where I can be found. Then I sit on top of the gas station guy's desk, drinking the soda he's gotten for me.

I think of what I will look like to her—some girl sitting on the desk in the Texaco that is lit up like a little frontier settlement on this foggy night in the middle of this place in the West, when we are still literally surrounded by cornfields and roads that go off into the night on the deepest blackest desert so you get the huge impending sense of what the pioneers encountered, those who walked two thousand miles only to arrive exactly *Nowhere*.

Though I cannot paint, I feel myself to be the inhabitant of some really lonely canvas. I'd have thought of a painting by Edward Hopper, had I ever seen one, but this is the American West, where we basically don't yet have books or paintings or many art museums, in that none of this is yet actually common, and what we have is the air and the sea and sky and everything that wasn't air or sea or sky was cast off and left in the muddy tracks of the wagon ruts.

Or I'd think of some other American painter—and it must be an American, since we're the best at this—who uses thick bands of raw pigment straight from the tube, so color's employed to make walls so high you can't see over them, and everyone's spaced just so along a certain grid, and light is actually then subtracted in order to describe what is, finally, a magnificent silence, which is what the universe actually thinks of us.

I see my aunt pull up in the station wagon that she prefers my cousins and I not drive, and I see the proud way she carries herself, the brittle set to her mouth, her handsome face. My aunt's cheekbones are elegant.

I go to the car and open the door, and she doesn't yell at me, and I sit down and she still says nothing. She has recently started wearing a huge clump of religious medals, one of which is the Virgin of Guadalupe that my father gave her one long-ago summer when he was sent to recuperate in Mexico at the home of the woman they call La Señora, one of the several times he cracked up.

My aunt brings her left hand to clutch her metals, which look like dog tags, then reaches over with her right hand. Her long fingers are tan, her fingertips are cold. Her hands are always fragrant from smoking cigarettes, a smell I happen to like.

She takes my hand in hers and closes her eyes in what might be a prayer of thankfulness, and when she opens her eyes I see that they're watering. This cannot possibly mean she's crying, since she and I are the same and we're stoic, as is my mother, also the other grandmother who's not a drunk. We're all Daughters of the Golden West and we all share these same tragedies, and these are griefs so huge they've long since served to dry our tears. I never cry and my aunt never cries, or if my aunt is crying, it'll take me years to find that out and years more to discover why.

7
Money Shot

WHAT IS BASICALLY most different about my generation is that we wear pantyhose. We're still required to wear dresses to school and cannot yet wear pants, but now—since pantyhose were invented—we can roll our skirts up at the waist so our knees show, roll them higher still so we expose whole areas of the flesh of our inner thigh, up into the shadows of what is hidden and what's never before been shown, and this has changed us not as a mere matter of style, but *fundamentally*.

What this means is, we are never going to have to turn out like *They* are, which shows not only in how we dress but in how we carry ourselves. By *They*, I mean our teachers, our mothers, our aunts, our grandmothers, who are repulsive, actually, if you stop to really think about it.

By *Them*, I mean *all* of them, *all grown-up women.*

When I am with my friends, I feel I've escaped into another country that in no way even pertains to *Them*. We feel we are inventing sex, as it has never occurred to *Them* and is a world that is ours alone.

I feel this powerfully: The rules of this country of ours, the one we will grow up to own, have changed, as has the language, and there are expanded boundaries for us that didn't apply to *Them,* and this shows most in how we talk, also in the striding way we walk. We no longer feel gagged and hampered, as if we can suddenly say the things that *They* would never even dream of thinking.

We may not yet have birth control, but we can feel it coming and it is coming right to us. We know these things without really knowing them, know them the way we suddenly know everything because we are the opposite of naïve, we are nothing if not *knowing.*

The news is electric. It's in the air; we pick it up by ant noise, and suddenly it all applies to us. The news says we're never going to be trapped as they've been in these little shitty lives of theirs that trip by petty pace from day to day so completely *pointlessly*: their driving the fucking tiresome carpool, their loading and unloading the fucking asshole dishwasher, their shopping at the stupid places where they buy their repulsive *ladylike* clothes.

We're never going to be stuck down into the Ozzie-and-Harriet, twin-bedded lives of American women in which they are told they both Do and Do Not like sex, equally and in the exact same measure, which is why they giggle at the word. Grown women who giggle make me so angry I want to stride over and slap their faces whenever they giggle behind their upraised hands, as if modestly. I *hate* giggling as much as I *hate* modesty.

This is what I imagine for myself: a world in which I can suddenly be able to *do* anything I want, which means my body will be able to follow my thoughts into far-flung places. I want to be able to go anywhere I can imagine going; to be able to follow my mind, which has already imagined itself out of here. I believe this means I will find my way to *freedom.*

My friends and I define ourselves in opposition to Them. My aunt tries to give me something someone, not my uncle, has given her—it's this filmy red thing to sleep in that simply perplexes my aunt, as well as making her slightly angry. Because it's insulting, I think it's probably one of my grandmother's twisted little gifts; its deep-down lesson is How to Keep Your Man, Though It's Probably Too Late Now. My aunt holds it out to me, as if to ask me what we should do with it.

I'm actually shocked. Even I know she would never wear anything that looks like this—it's *gross*, these see-through baby-doll pajamas that look like they're designed for a prostitute.

My aunt's too vexed and confused, so I'm the one to wad it up and walk it to the outside trash.

The giggling-behind-the-hand, baby-doll, half-virgin/half-prostitute cuteness thing is so *exactly* everything completely repellant.

They don't know what they're doing on this account because they're all twisted up in the Thou Shant's. My friends and I don't happen to care what God thinks, in that we don't believe in God, or if He does exist he should have known better than to come up with these *ridiculous* models, this *virgin* who has a baby (and my friends and I are like, We are *so totally* sure *that* did not actually happen) and her really faggoty-looking son. Their example is supposed to prove how spiritual we're supposed to be and that sex is bad for you.

My friends and I don't actually *think* so.

My friends and I are never going to be *repressed*. For one thing we're going to find things out, look stuff up for ourselves if *They* are too ashamed to tell us.

We poke around Cheryl's house and find the Kinsey Report hidden on the top shelf of Ted and Sylvia's closet, and we lie on their king-size bed to read it aloud back and forth, until this makes us think of Ted and

Sylvia doing it, which grosses us out, so we take the book out to the pool house, where Dougie and his little friends come to spy on us.

We intend to study up, become good at it. Jane Brown shows us what she practices with the younger boys she invites into her apartment after school, before her mother gets home from work. She demonstrates how younger boys can be controlled, how you have them lie atop you and you hook your legs behind their knees and spread their legs, which also opens you.

We practice this, also other positions. We read the words aloud, along with comic addenda and commentary, such as, Lick his asshole? And we say this *really loudly* so Dougie and his friends can hear.

That's so totally fucking *sick!* someone says, but we are able to say it, as *They* have never been able before to say these things without experiencing cosmic shame. Shame doesn't apply to us; shamelessness is part of the sheen in which we have wrapped ourselves.

We're going to actively allow sex into our lives, if only so we can shriek and laugh at what a fool having a human body tends to make of you. I look at the pictures in *Playboy* magazine with my cousin Jordy and his friend Paul—we've found it hidden in Dale Coffer's study while the grown-ups are outside by the pool, drinking their *cock*-tails, and why, I ask these boys, is it that drinks are named something like *cock*-tails, so they know I'm aware of their penises.

We three stare unabashedly at the huge jugs of the Playmate of the Month and her bright, invariably goldish hair, her dreamy eyes, her wet and slightly parted lips, while the three of us are lying on our stomachs right next to one another companionably. We're hiding behind the couch in the living room, then suddenly fighting and shoving—move *the fuck* over, you pervert, let me *the fuck* see—ready to shove the magazine under the couch if an adult comes into the room, which has grown dim in the twilight. I am older and I know more than they do already, and I take it away so I can read the letters to the editor aloud, especially the ones that say things like *oral sex* and *anal sex* and *climax* and *ejaculate*, saying this stuff aloud to gross them out, as they are—like Cheryl's brother—suddenly these *little* boys who have almost entirely been left behind by us.

Because my friends and I can say anything, we know we're *never* going to end up sitting at home, going nuts, smoking, drinking drinks during the Arsenic Hour, being counseled by the parish priest, who's in love with us but is too fucked up and repressed to swiftly step up to us and kiss us, as Father Bob should have done to my aunt, as she'd have made the best wife of an Episcopal priest the world has ever seen, which was probably even her destiny, which she refused—because of propriety—to step forth and meet, which is *a tragedy*, which is never going to happen to me.

We will never sit at home with our arms wrapped around ourselves as if to keep parts of ourselves from flying away into the universe, as my own mother did while becoming ever more isolated, more crazy, more lost from the Radiant Child she once was, the youngest-ever editor of *Pelican*, the humor magazine at Cal. My mom, who was once so obviously headed east, together with her best friends, Becky and Jo, to work at *The New Yorker* and conquer the Isle of Manhattan.

We will never be left home, locked in the house with umpteen kids, while The Men, who are firstborn and always six-foot-three and handsome and are therefore the most cherished creatures in our households, go out with whomsoever they want, driving off into the hot and glamorous night, whipping through the air in their new sports cars in badass colors.

This is our destiny: to not be withheld from our own destiny, and we will have birth control and we will own our *own* sports cars in badass colors, which we will drive with the top down and our *own* music blaring, and we will ourselves go out drinking with whomsoever we feel like and find *ourselves* in famous places, riding up and down in elevators with celebrities.

My friends and I will simply never turn out to be like the women in our neighborhood in the Valley, whose idea of being stylish strikes us as more and more grotesque, in that this includes wearing their hair in these ratted-up bouffant styles that are smoothed down, then pinned with infinite numbers of hairpins, then lacquered into place with hairspray. And they keep their eyebrows meticulously plucked—which is, like gardening, like washing up, yet another housekeeping chore—and their skin and nails are always perfect and their faces are held almost expressionless, as if they've been very expensively *burnished* of emotion, so you can't even come close to guessing what's on their minds.

Do the wives and mothers ever scream out during sex? I wonder as I lie outside in the darkest part of night, having climbed out my window to go stare at the stars from a chaise by the side of the steaming swimming pool, lights off, and I am thrilled to be by myself and in my wet underpants, thrilled—as I always am—to be where I am not allowed. I lie there listening to the night, but all I hear is cats making this ungodly noise, and it's because the males—or so it's rumored—have barbs on their cocks so the female can't slip off and get away.

My friends and I will simply never *become* these women whom we hate, who do not even resemble us, these women who have allowed themselves to be buckled into their cone-shaped bras so their breasts come to these weird, space age–seeming points, and whose butts are held taut and flat with girdles that have these strange, dangling-down clamps and devices that are supposed to clip together weirdly in order to keep your hose from sagging, so the whole underneath part of you is this bizarre feat of elaborate engineering that's obviously been designed to keep everyone's hands off you.

My friends and I are not like that—we feel ourselves and each other up.

Women's stuff is all weirdly menstrual and all about reproduction, and it's made of clamps and pads and rubber, and the bras and the underwear have this specific latexy, corsety smell that's like a scientific laboratory, or a hospital room, and so this is somehow the medicine we need to get *better*, and the Kotex we buy and then hide so the boys don't see them, girdles are the pink-plastic color of Band-Aids, which are supposed to look like skin but never had the slightest thing to do with the color of anyone's skin, as if the inventor of Band-Aids was too afraid to *look* at flesh without feeling that nakedness would make his eyes melt, and instead he went by the crayon in the box that was marked *Flesh*, another idea that has nothing to do with reality.

⬓⬓⬓

Our aim is always to wear as few clothes as possible, only two or three things. We need to be fast if we're going to get out of here. Everything about us is made for speed: Our short skirts are a direct challenge to the Powers That Be, so too our tight little sleeveless tops.

My friend Kat and I, who are on the girls' swim team, take long strides down the halls at school, brazenly lifting our eyes to those of the teachers who dare to stare at us. She's like I am, a half orphan, only it's her mom who's dead, so she's not well supervised. No one else has a name like hers, which is dangerous and therefore sexual because it's not traditional. Her name is actually Katherine, but she refuses to go by that, since this was her dead mother's middle name.

Kat and I have already been so deeply wounded, nothing else anyone does can touch us, which makes us almost impervious to harm. We encourage each other to act like this, becoming delirious with our own recklessness. She shows me how to shoplift. We go into a store, and while one of us—and we are monumentally self-possessed and exceedingly well spoken when we choose to be—engages the shoplady with this fake-adultish discourse, the other goes up and down the aisles, stuffing whatever she wants up the sleeves of the baggy hooded sweatshirts we wear after swim practice, or down the waistbands of our jeans.

We leave the store whooping, and the *lady*—and how I *hate* that word—knows she's just been so totally *had*. We whoop and scream as we run across the parking lot, as the shit we've stolen—which we don't even that much want—falls out of our clothes and we leave it there on the asphalt, which is even more *hilarious*.

People stare at us, we swear at them, we flip them off. We find ourselves on the highway, which is the abyss, as boys and men sense what we are, which is dangerous, and slow their cars to speak to us. We tell them to FUCK OFF and we walk out into traffic stopped at a light to walk along on the meridian divider, where we feel safe, going on down the middle of the highway like it's our tightrope out of here, and because we are propelled by tragedy—the early death of a parent—there is nothing to hold us here, so I feel that each of us may escape.

The world has never seen this thing before, though it has existed in the West—the American girl, the one who believes she can say or do anything and therefore feels untouchable.

We smoke cigarettes. Some of us can drive, and Kat and Jill and I all pile into Suzie's father's pink convertible Cadillac with its top down and drive to the beach with a paint-by-numbers canvas of Jesus' virtually life-size face riding along with us. We hold it in front of our own faces at a stoplight so that people glancing over will see that we've made a hole in the lips of Jesus with the point of a screwdriver just the size of a cigarette, so we can smoke through this hole in the life-size, paint-by-numbered face of Our Lord.

We end up in Malibu, where we pick up boys who are mildly shocked by us, which we find hilarious.

We are fevered, crazy, we feel like we're right on the verge of hysteria, and we've been good students in the past but now I am reprimanded in Honors English and am sent to the girls' vice principal for dress-code violations. I have to roll my skirt down from how I had it up at the waistband, and I get demerits for comportment; a couple more means a note home to my aunt, who will ground me. At lunch five or six or seven of us are made to kneel on a table to show that our skirts touch the tabletop; the teacher doing this hopes it will humiliate us, but we don't care and we comically contort ourselves to get our skirts to touch, and one of us, and this may be me, unzips her skirt to slide it down, and someone else leans way forward so her underpants show in back, and we are the opposite of humiliated because boys have begun crowding around to see, and now they look at us differently, and what *can* they do to us anyway—expel the whole tenth grade?

We feel hot to the touch, flushed with the day's excitement. The women at Sav-On stare at us as a group of us ding the bell to warn them that their store is being assaulted. There are now five of us, and while Kat and I, who are expert at sounding adult, talk to the ladies at the cash register, the others fan out in a way they cannot possibly keep track of. They aren't used to this kind of behavior from nice girls like we are, those who are white and who go to a good white school; we are these good white girls who are suddenly stuffing makeup and 45s down into our cutoffs.

It is *in defiance* of being good and because it makes these *ladies* feel oddly powerless.

We enjoy traveling in a pack like this, the group in which our individual identities are submerged, and the women stare as we move down the street in close and laughing clusters that are tantalizing but also keep us safe from men. The women stare as if we're very obviously conta-gious, like it's smallpox we're carrying, as the Europeans brought this kind of infectious disease to the New World with them and ruined inno-cence. These women know there is nothing they can do to protect those precious to them, those who are not yet inoculated by experience and who know no better than to be drawn to us, which would be their sons and husbands, and we're told about being *prick teasers* and the dangers to boys of *blue balls,* but we frankly don't give a shit.

We look like we're headed where some of us may be going, which is the freeway exit in a certain town in the Valley that's called Reseda but might as well be marked This May Well Be the Death of You, as this is where the girls who've come to California on buses from other places in the country end up when their other kind of movie dreams do not work out.

My aunt *knows* all this but can't imagine what to do. She's never had a teenage girl before, particularly one who likes the feeling of being balanced there on the rim of the world, getting ready to tightrope-walk off into complete nothingness because this girl has felt dead so long that anything that makes her scared will also give her the thrill of being alive, which is the opposite of the death-in-life she's used to.

As it happens, we live one town over from Reseda and we already know all these men in LAPD Vice, and one is the brother of my friend Mindy Dunnigan's father, Max, who works in The Industry but also makes his money in other, more predictably profitable ways.

My aunt uncannily knows exactly which of my friends are being well supervised. She believes Mindy Dunnigan's house to be what she calls "an attractive nuisance," so I am barely allowed to go there. She knows that on weekends, Max and Rusty Dunnigan take the smaller kids on their cabin cruiser and go boating over to Catalina Island, leav-ing Mindy home alone.

I'm not allowed to spend the night at the Dunnigans', so I lie and say I'm staying at Suzie's or Jill's or Cheryl's. Kat's is off-limits because of her no-mom thing, as is Jane Brown's because her mom is divorced and works.

I'm sixteen and I know nothing about The Industry, aside from the fact that it doesn't seem very glamorous, that it's full of the kinds of people my mom calls Sad Little Men. Some of our neighbors, such as short, dumpy, bald Mr. Weymeyer, who is in no way attractive, are members of the Academy and so get to vote for the Oscars. I also babysit for Henry Mancini and his wife, who live around the corner from us and have twins, but The Industry doesn't impress me because nothing impresses me, in that I'm in a lulled and shut-down state that may have something to do with either shock or grief, though *grief* or even *sadness* is not a feeling I'd typically describe myself as having.

More than anything, either I feel the plain dumb thing that is being numb to all feeling or else I feel strangely tingly and anticipatory, which is something I don't actually feel in my mind, but rather in various parts of my body. It is slightly terrifying to feel sexual—a set of feelings that are in the body and that lie, I find, right next to physical hunger, as both sit in the heavier organs of the belly and well below the heart.

Something, I often think, is *just about to happen.*

I get to go on dates, as long as my aunt knows the boy. One boy takes me over the hill to see *Goldfinger* in Westwood, then parks on Mulholland so he can kiss me, but his mouth tastes off, some strange milkishness, so I make him take me home. Sexuality starts out okay but then veers off toward Band-Aids, turning so quickly from desire to queasiness.

And it's true that I almost never like the boys who like me, including the senior who asks me to his prom, but for some reason I'm pressured to go, though I don't know anybody in that grade and I'm horribly ashamed and embarrassed to do the prom-type shit I all of a sudden need to be doing: going to Bullock's Wilshire with my Grandmother Delia to buy a really humiliating dress, having to buy grown-up underclothes, going to a beauty parlor to get my hair *done* in the kind of bizarre updo thing that makes me want to pound the face I see looking back at me in the car visor's mirror.

So I go right home, take all the hairpins out, and immediately wash it and dry it and wear it my regular way, which is rolled on huge rollers so it curves a little under but mostly hangs down straight.

The whole prom experience is excruciating. I feel like I'm getting hives in my throat, feel like I'm being asked to act like something I have no hope of ever being—that is, this happy, pretty girl who'd feel honored to be asked to go to someone's prom with him. I know I am in no way ready for this mess that so reminds me that it's this bizarre, ritualistic prep for the satin-and-silk part of getting married and being A Bride, the whole idea of which makes me almost physically sick—how the white is supposed to reference how everyone's all *involved* in your virginity.

In fact, though I can say any manner of swear word, aside from certain derogatory words for *woman* (*cunt, bitch, twat*)—which are, for whatever reason, particularly sanctioned not only in my family but also in my own mind—I can't stand certain everyday terms that reference one's status as a person who is not yet sexually active, at least to That Unknowable Degree.

I suffer from Word Magic, which is what primitive peoples who cannot really tell the difference between the word and the act this word represents have.

I can actually barely stand the word *virgin*, for instance, which creeps me out, or the term *bridal suite*, or the verb *consummate*, or even the name of a drink my uncle sometimes has on Sunday mornings after we get home from church, which is called a *Bloody Mary*.

The sound of these words are abhorrent to me, in that hearing them uttered makes me almost literally ill.

I associate all this with *brides*, with what is obliquely related to everybody's cultural expectation of a girl like me: that I'm supposed to meet someone and withhold my body from him, and this is to trick him into marrying me so I can wear this stupid white dress (which looks exactly like what a baby is christened in) that is made of yards and yards of satin and lace, which strikes me as simply tacky.

This very profound aversion I have to the entire concept of getting married may go back to a basic misunderstanding I had when I was small and my mother explained what she called the Facts of Life to me, which I understood, she told me later, as everyone watching two people in church have sex in front of the rest of the congregation.

෴

I'm sixteen. My friends and I know everything in our bodies and can say all words aside from the more normal ones having to do with matrimony, which sounds like a prison sentence, also other sickening terms, such as *mutual masturbation*, that we've read in Kinsey or in the sex manuals that turn up.

My friends and I at first know nothing about pornography, not even that it exists, though we live on the periphery of the vortex from which it swirls outward and is disseminated like sparks flying off a pinwheel.

Porn is being produced around us in warehouses and on soundstages all over the San Fernando Valley, and this is pre-video, so the porn part of The Industry still requires a motion-picture camera, film, and okay lighting, and film is really expensive and the whole thing costs *the earth*. Legitimate movie soundstages are used in the off-hours, so there's this other crew that comes around, and sometimes it's almost the same people who are moonlighting over here or sunlighting over there, working long hours and in grueling shifts. Sound, if it's used at all, is overdubbed, is only ever grunts and guttural moans, not plot lines, so porn can sell into any market, as these kinds of noisy cries never need translation.

And these actors and actresses are the same actors and actresses used in the real movies and commercials, those who came as if Los Angeles *beckoned*, since they were the best-looking girl or boy in their high school in Duluth, Minnesota, because California has *always* beckoned and drawn people forth to it, as the word itself has this magnetism and this promise that says you're just inches, really, from seeing your name six feet high and luminous.

As it was in my family in the Days of Yore, the word *California* will sound like destiny, but so far the doors of Twentieth Century Fox or Columbia or Paramount or Warner Brothers haven't opened up to you, and your agent has written this address on a little slip of paper and given it to you a little embarrassedly, and it's there off that certain exit in Reseda, a left turn and that quick right turn, and you find an unmarked back door to that certain warehouse because God knows you have to somehow pay the rent.

Besides, no one who knows you back in Duluth will probably ever watch these movies, which are still called *skin flicks,* as selling and buying them isn't part of a middle-class transaction and is still illegal, so even laying hands on a print of one of these requires knowing someone in Vice or someone else involved with the *underclass.*

I know about the underclass already because of my dad's run-ins with LAPD Vice. The word reminds me of the wild activity of sow bugs in the fragrant earth when you turn over a granite boulder.

Because these movies are really expensive, and your laying hands on one would depend upon your knowing someone who's well connected to this certain part of The Industry, someone like Max Dunnigan, who's a producer for commercials and has a brother named Frank who's a sergeant who works in Vice.

Even setting up one of these things to watch is really complicated in that you have to have an elaborate home-movie setup with a reel-to-reel projector and that kind of pearlized home-movie screen that flips over and pulls open from the top. Or you could tack a white sheet up on the wall of the den at the Dunnigans', which is an interior room that gets really dark.

Porn is still pure raunch, still plays to the most bestial of motives. There's nothing about it that says sex is a healthy part of the adult human experience.

This is pre–Mitchell Brothers of San Francisco, pre–*Behind the Green Door*, pre–*Deep Throat*, pre-Haight-Ashbury and our own hippie days, which will be this tiny window that lasts only a fraction of a second, and during which we will wear translucent dresses and tiny undies and no bras at all, and we'll be so totally stoned and dancing from shadow to shadow in the Panhandle, and convinced that no one would ever hurt us, that the day has dawned in which it's finally safe to be *a girl*.

So far, porn is almost entirely grim. Porn belongs to the underworld, and it speaks to the whore/pimp part of us, where everything is not as much about sex as you would think, and is actually more about money.

My aunt knows things aren't right at the Dunnigans', but she may not yet have a word for what's going on over there, except that her eyes flutter when we discuss it, which means her soul does not approve. She doesn't like or trust Mindy Dunnigan, who's been caught in the boys' wing of our house, making out with my cousin Graham, and my aunt's completely right when she thinks Mindy's probably one of those girls who's hell-bent on getting pregnant as a way out of her present circumstance.

Mindy is actually Max Dunnigan's stepdaughter, so she has a real father somewhere whom she's lost somehow, as I have lost my own. And my friends in high school have now, as a pattern, stopped conforming to the norm of the one mom and dad matched up and safely locked together in their chaste, twin-bedded Ozzie and Harriet lives.

I lie out in the backyard in the middle of the night and wonder whether women honestly do or do not like sex. I worry about what they think of it, that they can still—in the substance of their bodies—somehow remember how it was on the frontier that they were always, always pregnant, then often simply bled to death because of it.

Thinking about their grown-up physical bodies—the bodies of adult women (with all that secretly implied bloody stuff and the obvious risk of death implied in childbirth)—makes me queasy, in the same way as watery eggs.

The Ozzie-and-Harriet space-between-the-beds thing is simply confusing, in that it has resonance with my own experience, but I can't figure out if that resonance is even *real* or not. Do married people in other, more normal families *actually* sleep like this, and if so, what is *that* supposed to mean? The Ozzie-and-Harriet hiatus is also being laid down at the exact same moment in which the Kinsey Report is being read by my parents and my aunt and uncle and all their college-educated friends, who *act* like they're sophisticated, who are all trying to at least *act like* they are practicing heterosexuals, though they aren't—evidently—very good at it.

Because my friends' moms have started to be divorced, have started to work outside the house, as American women used to at least, before the 1950s got hold of them and told them to stay home with an apron tied around their waist and to live in the house with the White Picket Fence.

The Apron-Around-the-Waist trick is one sure way, as my mom has deduced from her superior vantage point of Ward G-1 in the State

Mental Hospital at Camarillo, to get whole hordes of women to completely lose their minds, which she tells me one of the times my grandfather drives Geo and me up to see her.

Beware, she tells me, The White Picket Fence.

Children are now growing up in what's called a "broken home," whose stigma, of course, also applies to me, though my own family situation at my aunt and uncle's is more complicated and hidden, in that the household looks so All-American and stable.

My grandmother is clear that vice doesn't come from *her*, though her blue-bloodedness has been polluted, of course, by her marrying my grandfather, scion of an American Dutch family whose lineage goes back to two drunken brothers so worthless that they were first thrown out of an entire (and, by the way, exceedingly drunken) country, given free passage from Holland to the New World, then tossed off a ship slightly upriver from what is now Troy, New York, in 1644. The *burgh*, or *hill*, in our august-sounding name comes from the slight rise in the land where they lighted, which, my father always said, was in all likelihood in fact *a midden*.

What we know about these brothers, Giesbert and Clyes, we derived primarily from their arrest records, in which they were constantly brought up on charges for public drunkenness or for fighting or for stealing each other's pigs.

And my mom makes sure we know that almost all American Vandenburghs are, in fact, descended from *both* of these two wastrel brothers, in that the same Henrys and Marys and Williams and Margarets kept intermarrying their cousins all down through generations and centuries, which concentrated the affinity for *vice* that we all seem to carry in our genes.

〇〇〇

My friend Mindy's stepfather is either deaf or, as is said, hard of hearing, so he bellows at us, but then, he bellows at everyone. He has a huge head with a shock of sandy hair that he wears longer than most men wear it, which may be his way of trying to cover his hearing aids, which are big, flesh-colored, and conspicuous. His manner is one of manic, joyful yelling. He's playful, always hollering, braying, in that rounded-off way of those who can't quite hear the way the rest of us bite down hard on consonants.

His yelling is only another one of the ways this household is different from my own, which is very High Church, as my mother says, which means it's staid and quiet and so nonconfrontational that no one ever argues.

Max is all *involved* with Mindy and her friends. He gets into the pool and plays watermelon football with us, but we know we need to stay away from him.

The deafness has a congenital element, so a couple of Mindy's half brothers or sisters are deaf as well. There are a lot of kids in the Dunnigans' somehow patched-together household, the seams knit by Mindy and her younger brother's having taken their stepfather's last name.

Their house is only a few doors from our high school and is a natural hangout that Max Dunnigan has outfitted with whatever kids might want. The Dunnigans' swimming pool is deeper than anybody else's and has a slide and a springboard. The rec room has a pool table and a soda fountain that Max keeps stocked with huge commercial tubs of ice cream, as well as cherries and chocolate syrup.

We all *know* about Max without anyone's telling us. Mindy makes the "he's crazy" loop around her ear and says, Fuck you, Max, to him at full volume when he's not facing in her direction. We know what's wrong without anyone's telling us, because you can't ride in the front seat of the car without his putting his big paw of a hand on the skin of your leg that shows below your cutoffs, and his is a man's hard hand, strangely textured, as if the whorls of his fingerprints are somehow exaggerated.

But we think of a person like Max as generally harmless—as a Funny Uncle, though our own uncle isn't one of this variety—and it's our conceit that we can *handle* him.

We know about Max instinctively, know too that we're important to him, that he values us, that we can get him to do things for us and give us money and rides here and there. We're sixteen, we don't have boyfriends yet and we don't really date.

We are suddenly powerful. Max Dunnigan in some way fits in with this, in that we now have the power to attract a man like this and the power to repel most women, and this means that we'll never have to go live in the house that sits behind The White Picket Fence.

⚇

I know all about all this stuff but still suffer from what feels like a very childish aversion, in that I honestly can't imagine really wanting anyone to fuck me.

I honestly mostly like kissing, but only the right boy. I like the power that being sexual gives me, his putting his hands on me in places that are not numb, but I don't want to be involved with this boy's dick, very frankly.

The times I do go ahead and feel his dick, I sense what he too feels: that his erection is bizarre, humiliating, that it *tells* on him, and what it says is that he's way more bestial than I am. A boy's erection is something that stands between the two of us and is in no way uniting.

But I do like kissing, as this is how I'm able to imagine which ones might turn out to be okay to go to bed with. *Going to bed with a boy* is the antique Ozzie-and-Harriet phrase that has replaced the one my mother uses, which is *sleeping with*. *Going to bed with* creeps me out slightly less than the other, more graphic terms do, which include *screwing, nailing, getting laid*. We don't yet call it *having sex* or *fucking*, and I haven't yet heard it called *getting busy, balling, jumping his or her bones*, or *doing the nasty*.

For me—with my gift of word magic and my very vivid imagination—kissing so totally *says it*. Kissing—as long as the boy smells good and tastes good—is like this little haiku of how the sex will be as soon as we get around to it, as kissing is like the sex *exactly*, how it will or will not be sloppy in the way of kissing a drunk boy, one who is inexact and noisy.

Kissing is the three-line note with all the pent-up nature of the real thing packed down into it. I'm really good at kissing, and if the boy smells good and tastes right and feels right, I withhold nothing. It has everything to do with smell and taste and fantasy, also with the really physical part that I more and more enjoy: all the softness, hardness, warmth, the texture of teeth and tongue, as if our souls are in our mouths and we can finally say the things that let us speak.

And kissing is, of course, what's missing completely from the movies Max Dunnigan sets up for us on the projector in the dark den at the very center of Mindy's house. I know about the economics because of Max and his brother, who works in Vice. We can easily overhear Max Dunnigan bellowing to his brother about this or that, and his brother shouting back to make sure Max can hear him, when they're getting drunk out by the pool, and why should they hide it, since no one's going to arrest them?

Because film and studio time are so expensive, there's this almost clipped, Charlie Chaplin-like, speeded-up rhythm to some of these movies, and the production values are all over the place because they've been made by all these different operations. Max's brother confiscates them in the LAPD Vice busts, then takes them to a warehouse that has an editing machine and a film printer, where they're copied before being turned in as evidence.

This is a giant joke between the two loud Dunnigan brothers out by the pool getting loaded—that Vice pervades everything at all levels of society, that it touches all of us.

It's Max who has set up the projector, as he has told us that we, being girls, are mechanically incompetent. When we come over to Mindy's to drink the Coke and Bubble Up that shoots from the armature of the soda fountain, he has it ready to go at the flick of a switch. I drink sodas at the Dunnigans' though my aunt doesn't allow us to ever drink what she calls soft drinks, in that they are, according to her, pure sugar, and we know she knows this kind of thing since she went to medical school.

Vice, I think, is what tells us about the activities that exist in the silence and hiatus defined by the space between the twin beds at Ozzie-and-Harriet's house. We don't want to know about Vice in our own lives because this embarrasses us. We so far have only the joking vocabulary with which to talk about sex. We think we are all virgins, in that none of us has had an actual boyfriend. We imagine we are virgins—though the word itself contains this very serious aspect of both tragedy and creepiness, in that it seems to say so much about our destiny.

The cock is so huge it tents the sheet and is found by the nurse who tiptoes in, as if not to wake him. This penis is strangely veined and old looking, unlike the boy penises of our brothers and cousins, which we've seen surreptitiously in getting in and out of swimsuits, and which are still what we think of as *clean*.

The lighting is terrible, so it's sometimes hard to decipher what you're seeing. The cock sticks out or it sticks up, and there is strange editing and confusion, and there'll be a couple of jittering cuts—with no narrative interlude or plausible explanation—and now the cock is being handled, now sucked. Now it is the mouth of the fully clothed nurse or waitress or secretary. The nurse or waitress or secretary sucks the penis for a while, then hikes up her skirt, climbs up on the man's body, and puts the penis inside of her, then rocks back and forth to ride it.

She rides it until she suddenly hops off. As the camera closes in on her face, she looks right at the camera and smiles. Then the penis starts to spurt come into her face through its little slit.

That's the Money Shot, Mindy says.

We all know she knows way too much about this, in that she's starting to earn money in The Industry. Last year she was working as a hand model, so her fingernails are always expensively manicured.

Wearing red fingernails, I somehow know, is a subtle sign of moral degradation.

Mindy earns money every time her hand is shown on TV reaching into the bowl to extract a potato chip. She mimes doing this. This money is called residuals.

We know nothing; we also know everything. We recognize this sex as gross, unattractive, and we say so to one another—that that guy's thing is just so fucking ugly—but we don't go home and we don't not come back the next week to watch the next one.

The movies, most of which are silent, show behavior that is aberrant, but we don't care. We are aberrant, if not in deed then at least in the wildness of our heated minds, which can think of all kinds of disgusting things that we might want to one day do or, better, watch as they happen to other people.

This is what the movies are trying to teach us: You let the cock come in your face. You smile like you're happy about it.

Or these movies may be about recruitment, I'm guessing, becoming initiated. The guy brings you to the warehouse where the film is made in order to pimp you out. This is The Boyfriend and he fucks you, but he wants you to fuck other people, too, while he is watching. He wants to see you do it. He wants you to do it with one, two, three other guys, all the guys in the warehouse.

Or a stable, a horse farm, may be involved. Can you do it with this many men for him? It's how he'll know you love him. Can you do it with the cowboy in chaps but no pants who beats you with a riding crop? Can The Boyfriend get you to let him do whatever he wants to you? Can he put you in the breeding crate while the little piglets, whose teeth are sharp, are suckling on your nipples?

The camera moves in on your face as the little animal teeth bite your nipples. Either The Boyfriend or the one he's pimped you to fucks you from behind. Your face, we notice, is deformed by what might be either pain or ecstasy.

That is so completely fucking gross, we say, but we do not not watch. We in fact watch movie after movie until we're strangely expert and can tell exactly when it's just about time for the Money Shot.

Will you do it with six convicts if The Boyfriend asks you to? Will you do with Mexicans? Will you do it with Negroes?

Are you willing to become his *thing*? these movies seem to ask, the one pure thing that no longer thinks or questions or needs to speak, that is only cunt to his cock, so he is cock completely and solely.

Would you whore for him? Would you stand on the street corner in a shitty part of Hollywood in the cold, wearing mascara that drips like you have been crying, and give him all the money you get for it? Is there no part of you he couldn't fuck or have some other man fuck if he asked you to?

The movies might be training, I'm guessing, on how to go out into the night and become one with Vice, to actually join up, as my mother says my father did, to stop thinking about these things and actually go and do them.

We might be being trained by Max, I guess, whom I now trust less and less, as there is something deeply wrong with a man who'd set these movies up for his teenaged daughter and her friends, and even though he's not there watching them with us, his presence is all around us.

Obedience is the moral lesson of these movies, which is strange because they appeal to the parts of us that are utterly unruly. We think we can handle boys, men, anything that comes to us. The movies say we need to learn a lesson.

⸬

Boys never come to Mindy's house. We are girls only, are—I'm only guessing—virgins, and we kiss each other and suck one another's nipples but call it practicing and stay uninvolved.

There is something so odd and inconclusive about what passes for sex in these days in the San Fernando Valley, and I'm guessing that sleeping with one boy might not even do it when it becomes time for me to get rid of my virginity; I might have to fuck one boy, then fuck another—maybe a whole raft of them—in order to get rid of it, and I want it gone, its whole virgin, white-satin, bloodstained creepiness.

I don't know the boy who seems to be *up to this*.

⸬

My aunt disapproves of Mindy's parents because they let us drink soft drinks and eat ice cream, and because they are not educated.

I always know who is and isn't educated based on my aunt's enthusiasm about my going over to whichever of my friends' households, as if a college education is the wall that needs to stand between our exalted selves and crass vulgarians like Mindy's parents, with their sweets and porno.

Rusty Dunnigan is a lunatic mom of a variety I've never before encountered. She's a disaster junkie who listens to police band radio provided by the Dunnigan in Vice. She regularly runs out to her station wagon without saying a word, leaving the little kids to us, and gets in to go drive to the scene of an accident. She collects pieces of the wreckage, taillight glass from a fatal car wreck, metal from an airplane crash. She keeps these in a special place in her closet, goes to get them if you act the slightest bit interested, and will tell you all about the scene as she came upon it.

She says it with a rapt, trancelike look on her face that tells you she's completely transported, her vision fixed on the cataclysmic moment, and I somehow know—though I'm actually too young to know this—that sex is somehow equal to disaster, equal to blood and death.

〇〇〇

The lesson of pornography, at least as I am taking it in, has to do with whether or not you prefer sex to be involving. You can stay out of it altogether, as if you were the woman being fucked, who looks at the camera and smiles as come splurts over her face in the Money Shot.

This is what I already know, though I have no way of knowing it: You can be a drug-addicted hooker and still be a virgin, in that it is possible to have sex *all the time*, while in your soul that resides in your mouth and comes alive only by Word Magic—in the saying of a beloved's name, for instance—who you really are doesn't necessarily participate.

The movies are brute in that they tell us what matters biologically: For the species to go on, you have to get the cock to come. The cock has to come. When the cock comes, the movie ends, as film and studio time are expensive. There is no plot to the stories except for that most ancient one—that it hardly matters whether or not the girl comes, whether she's enjoying it or is completely faking, so all that remains a mystery.

The cock comes, the action stops, and the film runs out, as there are no credits or trailers. The screen goes white. The projector makes the *clickety-clack* as the film comes off its sprockets.

000

The first time I ever have an orgasm, it's accidentally and completely noncontextual, while doing floor exercises in dance class for PE, a maneuver that asks us to straighten our legs, point our toes, then bounce our bodies forward toward our knees, and I totally know what this is because I am in no way mentally chaste. I'm not even interested in my own virginity and in no way value it, and if I could I'd just somehow skip over this piece of what has to happen or otherwise get around it, without having to go through *all that*, which is what my mother would no doubt call it.

My mother has somehow tutored me to be careful with boys, who aren't as tough as girls. This has to do with childbirth, and with the long road west, which makes Our People, by which she means girls and women, stronger, more solid at the core.

This is what I have, so far, to go on: Men and boys are a different kind of beast whose self-esteem is tied up in the size and shape of what I'll later think of as their Unit. White men and boys are particularly sensitive about this aspect of their anatomies, my mother either outright says or at least intimates, so we must never act to diminish them, as they've already been, she says, somehow diminished.

All the boys in my family have been circumcised. Boys are afraid, my mother says, because they've been circumcised, because they still hold in their infant memory the image of someone's coming at them with a pair of scissors or a bright and shining knife, which is why we are not to *criticize* men and boys, as—very honestly?—they're probably doing the best they can.

Boys, for instance, worry constantly that their penis and balls *can* fall off while they're sitting on the toilet seat, my mother says, a worry that—believe it or not—never entirely goes away.

These are the lessons I've learned about the Facts of Life. Men and boys are babies, my mother says, so we indulge them. You can fuck as many men as you can find, but this won't necessarily involve your psyche. Men and boys do much of their thinking with their cocks. Their cocks are what make men and boys *act up,* but it's the cocks that are doing this, so men basically cannot help it, which is what makes us fundamentally better than they are. Everyone actually wants the same thing, which is to get the cock to come, which is when everything settles down and becomes normal again.

Years later, a song I love captures the feeling exactly: We are fever, we are fever, we ain't born typical.

My mother's wisdom drifts back to me: You check the box marked *Other.*

8

A Continent of Grief

So NOW MY Uncle Ned is anyway turning out to be a *cad* or *lout* or *bounder*. He's what my mom calls yet one more *Good Time Charlie*, and this is widely known in our family, though it is never spoken of.

My diagnosis? That he's as sick of grief as he is of the rest of us, so he's obviously voting in favor of his own happiness.

He's sick too of this big house with its wings that reach out and around, as if to snatch up all light and air. The house is being perpetually *added onto* yet remains too small and crowded with the unruly energies of all us kids, who are lately climbing out of windows into the hot dry night, fragrant with humus in the planting beds and the chlorine vapor rising off the swimming pool.

Which is to say, my uncle's jealous, knowing it is Graham and Jordy and I who'll escape from here most soon.

And it's anyway just one more summer's day in the baking heat of what he calls the Rat Race, and the air-conditioning's running continually, so he yells at us again and again, Slide that door closed behind you! Do you think I want to pay to cool the entire neighborhood?

Late afternoon fading into evening, the Arsenic Hour, in which they sit in the cool underwater light of my aunt's blue-and-green color scheme to have yet another polite but tense conversation, and all he's thinking of is how he's *got* to get out of there, drive away, go do something he really *wants* while there's still time.

And the thin marine light reminds him of church, of my aunt's good works, her piety, the seriousness of her purpose, all of which oppresses him. She's ten months older than he. He's begun to say aloud, It's what I get for falling for an older dame.

The suburbs. They're flat, monotonous . . . he hates it here, and I actually know this feeling, too, know how you might just have to strike out with your clenched fists and smack the front windshield of the VW that you're riding in as a passenger. My uncle's lately driving a VW Bug, so he sometimes gives me a ride to school when my schedule conflicts with Graham's. My uncle's driving this car because it makes him feel like less of what he calls an Old Goat. My uncle says *Old Goat*, then snorts.

Uncle Ned is in his late thirties. When my father died, he became the oldest adult male in our family, aside from one agéd grandfather on my mother's side, who—by Poor Mouthing, by invoking the Power of the Weak—has managed to contribute nothing to the upkeep of the three bedraggled, half-orphaned urchins.

My uncle, in inheriting my two brothers and me, is now financially responsible for a wife and seven children.

What does my uncle do? He goes to his investment club—they meet at lunch, so they call themselves the Brown Baggers. He becomes more and more successful at everything he touches.

He's more cheerful than he's ever been, something my aunt notices. He travels out of town more often and when he's in town drives his new car away from home as soon as he can and stays away as long as possible.

And his cheerfulness makes odd but entire sense to me when I come at it slantwise, not with my mind, but by thinking with my body. I understand his happiness in the deep way I now know certain other things: that you can, for instance, get the boy you're making out with to press on your belly right above the pubic bone when you need to pee, and the sensation is completely thrilling, in that you retain your power and your modesty, not letting him touch your breasts or skin, and that you can stop him, stop him just short of ecstasy, and the whole time he actually has no idea what he's doing.

This is what my aunt often says about a boy: *You poor dear dumb thing.*

My uncle wants to drive around in a new car with the windows down, zipping through the chunks of hot, sagey night that waft through the canyons on his way to Malibu, voices baffling wildly, then snatched away. There to sit with someone glamorous who *wants* him, who's paying attention just *to him,* who is enveloped with him in a dark cocoon of secrecy, eating with him in a booth in a seafood restaurant where he sits on the banquette and feels his heart expand, pounding to fill his chest, all the blood he owns crying, *Rise up! Arise and be free!* And she slips her shoe off and puts her stockinged foot in his lap, where he cradles the silk heel of it, and as they turn to watch the sun go down, he says simply, because he's a simple man, You make me very happy.

And as he drives away from the too-thick-with-grief air of the house that is crammed with just too many of us, he figures he *gets* to do this, as an American male of the Upper Middle Classes, because American males of his generation are taught to think they are entitled to such privileges, to an expectation of happiness. Happiness has begun to seem like a destination to him, a place that lies elsewhere. He needs to go there while he still can, he knows, to this place where he'll be able to somehow *enter.*

Because everyone who's been in the West for any time has his or her own sad story, and the tragedies—I can't help but notice—become hinges in the narrative, places where the story turns. This shift—once accomplished—sends the tale in a new direction. Tragedy, I notice, has a way of rhyming with itself or doubling, like my uncle's Republican investment club's principle of interest always being *compounded*.

Uncle Ned's grief is different from my own, only in that it's *his* story that this family is always trying hardest to keep from telling.

And his personal grief anyway so completely trumps anything any of the rest of us can come up with, that any of us have—as my uncle says—to *moan and groan about*. His story is so tragic, it lies like a great archaic continent that's been buried by Geologic Time, whose evidence is seen only in the jagged strata of the Overthrust Belt, rock slices shoved diagonally upward and that make no sense, and are therefore perfectly inexplicable to all but the most learned of scientific eyes.

The continent of grief underlies all of our lives, I'm finding, but it is studiously ignored in this part of the family, while my own mother—who, it's said, *indulged* her grief and was therefore *driven crazy* by it—will speak of nothing else.

My uncle's story is such ancient history, I have no memory of who it was who even told me about it, though it must have been my mother, since she's the one who will *not* not say whatever occurs to her to say, this being one of the main reasons she's been committed to a mental institution.

As her father says, Margaret, women do not talk like that.

To which she answers, Dad, honestly? Really? They *do too*.

The shape and nature of my uncle's grief is the story that's been buried since he was about the ages Graham and Jordy and I are now—fourteen, fifteen, sixteen—when he was away at boarding school. This is when he lost his mother, sister, and brother in a hotel fire. It was in his school's town. They'd come to visit him.

This grief, which I figure must inform everything my uncle does, is simply so huge that he can't bear to acknowledge it.

And my uncle, who is my aunt's husband and therefore not related to me by blood, is unlike the rest of us in this one very fundamental way. He's a Western *man*, so he somehow manages to keep the oxcart moving, to stand by his dad to bury the dead and *who knows where?* since this is the West, where we burn the markers as firewood.

Tall men. Each tall man turns, with his back straight and his upper lip stiff, and these two are Edward Snowden Junior and *the Third*. To do otherwise would be undignified.

My uncle makes a point of being optimistic, forward-thinking. This pays, he says, when you're a Republican and a businessman.

My uncle's smart but he isn't deep. He's also *proud* of not being deep. He'll tease me about it, saying it's possible in this life to be so deep that you completely lack a surface.

He says this to me as I'm reading Shakespeare aloud to myself, sitting in the kitchen alcove, waiting for the wall phone to ring, hoping it'll be some boy I like, and wanting to head off Geo or any of my boy cousins, who will, having nothing better to do, race to answer it.

Five fathoms deep my father lies, I read beneath my breath.

I never liked Shakespeare, my uncle says as he's digging through the refrigerator. He's hungry, he's looking for something, because he *wants!* he *wants!* he *wants!* He must scroll past old food, push beyond the half-eaten sandwiches my aunt makes Geo and Thomas save for later, for when they're hungry and are begging for a snack. He must get beyond the vet-pack part of the fridge, the special dalmatian medicine that's kept in there for Murphy's hot spots. The fridge is also the reptile and amphibian supply store, so he must sort through canisters of moths and mealyworms to try to find anything vaguely appealing to a human.

That's okay, Uncle Ned, I tell him kindly. Shakespeare doesn't like you either.

My uncle and I are fond of each other, though I have no idea why; we're as unalike as night and day. But we have the orphan thing in common, also that we're tough in some profound way, as each of us recognizes in the other. I admire his talent for happiness, while he likes what he calls my *joie de vivre*. But I'm almost painfully observant, while my uncle purposely will not notice things and so comes off as an anti-intellectual clod.

I have certain strengths, in that I'm not like Geo, whose plight now troubles everyone.

The truth about you, my uncle says, is that you're a strong swimmer. Not fast, but you continue to plod along—it's the steady pace that'll get you where you're going.

I'm a strong swimmer, but I am also like my parents. Being like my parents—this is wildly praised as *creative* or *brilliant* or *hilarious*, then right away derided as *alcoholic, outré, self-destructive, crazy*—is just flat-out exhausting. It makes me want to go to sleep and not wake up—not to die, just to get a rest from the constant yammering.

My being *artistic* makes me act in a manner my uncle thinks of as contralogical. He's a Republican, a guy, and the highest value for a man like this is a) to win or b) if you can't win, to at least save yourself from drowning.

When a riptide catches you, therefore, you need to know that you must swim patiently sideways, without panicking, swimming parallel to the shore until the current releases its grip on you. Even the strongest swimmer will be overwhelmed trying to swim back to shore against a rip as strong as the ones we know.

My father, who had his own sailboat from an early age, taught me another way. You may also save yourself, he said, if you relax entirely into the current and allow it to carry you out to sea. You float on your back, look up, admire clouds, become one with the cawing seabirds—you see them well and enjoy the ride and in this way come to completely know that life will finally prove to be much too much for each and every one of us.

I've let this happen, let myself be carried out to sea beyond the break line, knowing I am a strong enough swimmer that I can get myself back to shore. My uncle doesn't get why anyone would allow herself to go *backward*, and I can't explain this to him, the simple pleasure of sometimes allowing yourself to submit to the backward pull.

It's because he doesn't really get Shakespeare, how the witches warn Macbeth yet Macbeth still goes ahead and does the exact thing he's been warned against, because it's his fate to do that, so he's therefore drawn toward his own future. And he goes directly there because he really just can't *not*.

My uncle is Republican. It's Republican to think grim fate is what happens to the darker, angrier races.

I, who am contralogical, was born having to live my life in a manner that feels retrograde to Uncle Ned, as if, though I am still a child, I am somehow fundamentally older than he is. I understand the undertow, that he and I are passing each other on our separate ways out of here, I'm growing up even as he struggles to stay young.

I live in his house, eat his food, and am not a Snowden—not, therefore, his blood, which is somehow English. I'm a girl, a teenager, and sort of Dutch, and he's never had one of these before.

And I can't explain myself to him: that I was born in obverse, facing history by going in the wrong direction, and I look back into Deep Geologic Time because this *comforts* me.

My job is to memorize the lives of my dead and still-living relatives, and to keep them with me not only by bundling them up and dousing them with camphor, but also by remembering their lines so people will know which *roles* they played.

My mother talks a lot about *roles* these days, because this is how the people in her group therapy in the mental hospital have been taught to express themselves.

∭

It is 1963, and part of what my uncle does with grief has to do with Edward Snowden the First, his grandfather's being English. The English are, as my aunt and uncle's friends Michael and Sarah Burlingham say, a cold, stiff, and ultimately disappointed tribe— disappointed because they believed they were God, but it turns out they aren't—which the Burlinghams should know since they were born in London.

I'm always wondering what people like the slaveholders or the British, who went out to conquer the world, did with all their guilt, because I know guilt to be the cause of things. Guilt will cause the turn in the narrative, become the elbow in the story that says *this* happened, then *this* happened *because* of that first thing's happening, which is what we're shown in *Crime and Punishment*.

My uncle, who doesn't like Shakespeare, also doesn't *go by*—as my mother would say—Dostoevsky, in the way my own parents always have. Your father, my mother says, was pure Fyodor Mikhailovich, while my life is turning out to be much more Émile Zola.

But anyone who reads *Crime and Punishment* can feel how the two events—the crime of Raskolnikov and his being punished for it—are magnetized to each other across countless pages or invisible time or even a mass migration across an entire continent.

There is simply no chance that anyone's going to get away with it.

His mother, brother, and sister—which was *everyone*—dying in a hotel fire, and their only being in that hotel when it burned because they were visiting him? How can my uncle live with this?

My own father's crime was to have not been speaking to his parents when his dad—on a trip to Illinois to see certain cousins—died suddenly, of a cerebral hemorrhage.

Historians call sudden-death-from-a-cerebral-hemorrhage-while-off-in-Illinois-while-visiting-certain-cousins a *Contingent Event*. The California Gold Rush is cited as one of the Contingent Events of the Civil War, in that the financial institutions to which all that gold was shipped were in the North, so those billions of dollars of wealth went there to be used by the Northern bankers to invest in the factories that manufactured munitions for the Union Army.

And because I don't understand what people like my uncle do with their guilt—that his mother, brother, and sister died in the fire *while visiting him!*—I imagine he must be magnetized to its having happened, so I study him for signs of it.

It happened in a beach town somewhere south of us. The school sits—or so I'm forced to imagine, since he won't speak of it—on a hillside above the town. I imagine that the boys in their dorms, awakened by the sirens, would have gone to their windows in their nightclothes to see the embers being carried upward and back, past the tops of the eucalyptus trees planted around the grounds as windbreaks. They might have thought to worry about the trees, which carry such a huge fuel load that they sometimes burst into flame with a tremendous *whoosh* that sounds like a bomb going off.

But my uncle is a firstborn boy, his dad's heir, a charmed boy in a culture that worships boys. He's tall, good-looking, very confident. My family has long been adept at producing such men. Each woman is then raised to marry a man like this in order to have more sons like these.

So my uncle might have imagined himself to be lucky, even blessed. He was a man among men, and high up in what my mother calls the Mucky Muck, which is the Great Chain of Being, the English being anointed as maybe the luckiest race there'd ever been, until the Twentieth-Century White American Male was *finally* invented.

So my uncle, gazing out of the dorm window, would *never have imagined* that the bells of distress being rung in the mission of that seaside town were, that time, being rung for him.

◊◊◊

I'm reading, which is *allowed* on a Saturday morning, but my uncle comes in from their rooms in the adult wing of the house and makes a goofy face at me to mock my being studious. He thinks I'm studious but I'm not, as that would require being systematic and even organized in what I'm reading, and I am honestly neither. Instead, I read because a good story is the best way to escape from wherever it is I am.

Dontcha wanna go do something outside in the living daylight? my uncle asks.

Nope, I say. I talk through the mouth I can hardly open since my chin's resting on my hand.

Why not?

Can't, I say.

Can too.

Don't *want to*, then?

Why not?

Depressed, I say and glance up at him. I invoke the word though I'm in the wrong part of the family to say this, as this is the portion of the collateral descendents of the blah-blah-blah, Holland Society, 1644, so forth, that doesn't *go by* what my mother calls The Psychological.

All the more reason to get going, my uncle says. Get off your *bee-hind*! Go change your shirt. Isn't that the same shirt you were wearing last night?

No, I say.

Looks the same.

It isn't a *shirt*, Uncle Ned, I say. It's the top to my pajamas, I wear it *all the time*, and now I'm wondering how it can be that he's *only now* noticing.

Your pajamas? he asks. At eleven thirty in the morning? Where's your aunt?

Dunno. I say. Food shopping? Altar guild?

I mean it, he says. Go get dressed.

Noooooo . . .

Yesssss, he says, and while you're at it, brush your hair.

But I don't *want* to . . .

I don't *care* if you don't want to. My uncle says this through a blaze of straight white teeth, grinning as he speaks. Get going, he says. Go out and ride your bike. You and Jordy take the little guys. Ride to town, buy them all an ice cream.

Then my uncle takes out his wallet, from which he extracts a neat little fold of cash and begins peeling off bills. Money's new, bills feel sticky as he hands them to me, and the smell is loud with ink.

And since my uncle is as famously generous as my aunt is tight, he then remembers the others, who might want some of his money, and so heads in the direction of the boys' part of the house, calling, Did everyone get his allowance?

At the door to the kitchen he turns to grin at me, saying, I am a river to my people.

〇〇〇

I sulk and wear my pajamas around the house and won't wash my face or brush my hair, but only until something fun presents itself to do, in which case I can snap out of a pout in less than two seconds. My mother does not respect this quality of mine, that—depressed as I am and almost entirely defeated—I'm still eager to participate. I can even go somewhere sometimes and not completely hate it, go there and be almost entirely enthusiastic, which my mother really hates, since she and my father became almost curdled by their joint cynicism and she carries it on to this day, out of loyalty to him.

In my mother and father's lineage of our once august family—we're supposed to imagine given the grim state of the world—that committing suicide is a very rational thing to do, which I two- to three-fifths believe.

But now I live in a more or less normal house and have normal clothes and friends. I get dressed for school, then go out to the car and am carried along by the buoyant sense of my own weightlessness, having been released from the penitentiary.

Graham drives me and Jordy to school, and sometimes Cheryl DeCinces or Debbie Poor, everyone sitting on everybody else's laps. It's only cute girls, those Graham says are bitchen, who get to ride in our car.

We're teenagers. We're porous. We're like the chalk you dip into vials of stain in chemistry and allowing someone non-bitchen to ride in our car with us might taint us with their weirdo-ness. Our status as human beings is actually so frail even walking down the hall *next to* someone non-bitchen is enough to *implicate* you.

The car still smells vaguely of vodka barf from when Graham took it out and got *boozed up, creamed, schooled in the fine art of drunkification,* on the first weekend he was allowed to drive it, so the car now stinks mostly only when the heater's on.

So going to school is like being on parole and I'm good in school and it's fun for me and my classes are almost always interesting. My teachers encourage me, which may be only out of pity for all my assorted tragedies, as I'm so completely unlike my uncle that everyone almost immediately knows everything about me—I don't care, as saying this stuff is becoming more and more who I am intrinsically.

Every part of school is fun, even the complaining about the asshole teachers, even completely hating it. I'm really good at hating things. My parents were *anti* this and that. It's Lina who says this, pronouncing it *AN-tee*. Lina's my dusty grandmother, not Delia, but the one who grew up raising pigs and flyfishing on a ranch in Montana.

It's in Mr. Greenbaum's first-period Honors English that I am asked to go first one Friday in November when our oral reports are due.

I'm surprised but it's okay, because I'm prepared and I've worn something okay to school and my hair's all right, so there's nothing really that obvious that's wrong with me. I've always looked like such an essentially ordinary person that it's a shock to everyone—myself included—to have to witness the ways in which I'm not.

My major problem—the language of which I'll find out later, expensively—is that I am not *well integrated*.

So I go to the front of the class, confident enough of my bitchenness, with my skirt rolled up at my waist to show the right amount of thigh, which is not permitted but is allowed, and I smile as I stand at the podium and put my report there in front of me and look at Mr. Greenbaum, who's sitting in the back and reminds me of my father—but then, every man I'll ever meet who is in any way good or nice or smart or kind will remind me of my father. Then I begin to speak, when I notice that my upper lip feels strange, and I understand that this is because it has started twitching.

And because I am not *well integrated*, this happens without my experiencing any conscious sense of my own nervousness, and so this comes as a complete shock to me.

And this isn't some barely perceptible tic—rather, it's this huge, very visible twitch that I can both feel and see. I'm witnessing the horror of it on the faces of my friends, who drop their eyes, too embarrassed by my bizarre behavior to even look at me.

This twitch, which raises my upper lip in the way of a snarl, continues the whole time I'm giving the report. I stand there and I continue speaking, and because I'm already a good writer, it's probably eloquent. It's probably eloquent and is probably about Hell, because we're reading Dante's *Inferno*. I can write about Hell knowingly because I've lived through much worse things than this, but as I continue to give this report, I know this just may be the incident that defeats me.

After today, I already know, I'll be so un-bitchen that even *my own cousin* won't let me ride in the car with him.

I'm going to have to go home and beg my aunt to change schools, to transfer to Reseda or Chatsworth or enroll at Marlborough, the exclusive girls' school in L.A. where Grandmother Delia went, though then I'd have to wait for her to get drunk, then beg her to pay for it, get her to sign something, so she wouldn't take back having agreed to do it.

And Mr. Greenbaum, for reasons I don't get—since he's as kind as my father was, and I was my father's favorite child—allows me to stand there with my face twitching the whole time I'm presenting my six to eight minutes on Hell.

Hell, as my dusty grandmother says, is always *other people*.

I've studied the architecture of Hell, so I know that the seventh circle of the seventh level is where they put all the betrayers, Judas Iscariot, as well as all other suicides. And Mr. Greenbaum, whom I liked and who I thought liked me, has me continue to stand in front of the room while my performance is discussed.

What's the first thing we noticed? he asks.

That she was nervous? someone says.

Really?, I think.

And how could we tell she was nervous?

And now my face, which is no longer twitching, has become hot, wet and red, and it occurs to me that I may cry, though I haven't cried since I was nine years old and my father died, as your father killing himself is the sort of numbing event that will actually anesthetize you, so my teenagerhood is probably turning out to be way less worse than it might be for a more normal person.

My tongue feels really fat. I bite my lips, which are also swollen. My hands are blotchy, I see, and these are hives—I've never had hives before but will, from this moment on, be sporadically afflicted. I can't actually speak as the class continues its discussion of the anatomy of my embarrassment.

And I'm still speechless with humiliation at the end of the period so I take my time gathering my books after class and don't leave with my friends, who go on without me as I dawdle, maybe wanting to spare me the shame of talking about this incident or, more likely, not wanting my twitch-lip thing to spread to them.

The class is in a portable, with a door and stairs on either end. The main benefit of being in a portable, away from the main building of the high school, is that these rooms open to the outside and don't trap the goopy, boiled-cabbage-and-canned-spinach-trapped-underwater seagrass smell of the cafeteria, which is so bad some days it's like we're being gassed.

Mr. Greenbaum is now thronged by over-anxious students who still give a shit about their grades, and who have gone up to him to get pointers on how to get a hundred—I so long ago stopped caring about *how to get a hundred*. I go down the back stairs. He comes to the porch of the trailer and calls to me, but I won't turn around. I'm too busy wondering if I can get transferred out of there and into Miss Lowenson's.

My next class is Mechanical Drawing, at which I'm excellent, maybe the best student in my section. I actually love the way this class requires us to draw some plain and uncomplicated thing, just this manmade object that is completely straightforward and in no way surprising. We must draw it from all angles and very precisely. I don't care that this isn't creative—I actually hate being creative, which only makes me more like my weirdo parents. All we must do in here is accurately render a metal plate or a four-inch bolt. Drawing like this is the most simple, meditative thing to do, and accomplishing it makes me feel profoundly peaceful.

I can go into this class and sit on my high stool at my tipped-up desktop and become entirely lost in the process of seeing this bolt, or whatever, really clearly and from every angle, and drawing it, then checking the measurements and proportions. I'm also working on my print handwriting, developing a technical hand that is blockish and neat and looks amazingly like that of my architect father.

I'd be entirely happy to stay in this class forever if it weren't for the boys.

Because of my brothers and my boy cousins, I am already completely used to boys, used to being treated, in fact, like a kind of honorary boy on the many occasions when I'm the only girl. This class, however, is made up of a different breed of boy: These either are stupid or have something else deeply wrong with them, in that they don't know how to be friends with girls.

What they do instead of taking on the assignment is waste their time trying to bother me, when this is the actual truth, which they're too fundamentally dense to realize: When your father kills himself and your mother gets sent to a mental institution, some jackass boys teasing you in Mechanical Drawing simply doesn't climb very high up the pain scale.

And their teasing isn't even clever; it's only *organized*, which means they're ganging up so that I can't glance past them toward the teacher without seeing all four of the boys in the row sitting opposite me, staring at my chest.

Boobs, one says.

Knockers, another whispers.

Jugs, one adds, and they're not talking to one another, which would make them turn their heads to the side, a movement the teacher might see. Instead, they're directing their comments at me.

Fucking assholes, I say, loudly enough that the teacher hears my voice, which is conspicuous because it's the only girl's voice, so it seems to float and carry. But the teacher has heard me, he more than likely can't believe it, so he asks me to tend to my work, which is consistently excellent, so he doesn't want to get mad at me. I'm still blotchy from the humiliation of Mr. Greenbaum's, and now I have to sit opposite these morons, who are basically too fucking stupid to live, and the one good thing about going to Marlborough would be that it's a girls' school.

I'm nauseated and I have hives in my throat, and I'm thinking I really do need to go to the nurse's office to get her to call my aunt to say I need to go home. Meanwhile, I use my fingers to comb my hair over my left hand and arm so it makes a curtain, I lean forward with my hand cupped like a visor to shield my eyes, and I look only at the sheet of paper that's masking-taped to my drawing board, and so make myself entirely calm as I enter my work.

Entering this work, or any work, is like becoming an atomic part of it, small to the point of being almost infinitesimal, so you are within the project and thus able to see the most itsy detail to the exclusion of all else around you.

I work, and all the while I keep my face down and my body hidden so they won't be able to catch sight of me.

〇〇〇

We're barely settled in third period—Señor Gallegos has taken roll and collected homework and is only beginning our lesson—when the principal comes on the PA to announce that President Kennedy, while riding in a motorcade, has been shot in Dallas, Texas.

Señor Gallegos is so stricken that he cannot speak to us. He simply sits down at the table in front of the class, holding his face in his hands, and we, who are embarrassed by this emotion, become completely quiet. Honestly, this room becomes quieter than any room I've ever known. It has something to do with the potential for all the noise that might come from thirty high school kids, and with our stifling any need to be loud or boisterous, we who are completely unaccustomed to being this quiet for long periods without direction, which only further emphasizes how quiet it is.

One person yells from outside in the hallway, but the whole school has been unnaturally muted, like a TV with the sound turned down.

This is the part of the sixties that is still almost exactly like the fifties, so children are still obedient, and though we're teenagers we still imagine we must obey our elders, so we are faced forward, hands clasped, silenced not by the enormity of what is happening to President Kennedy—or maybe to our whole country—but by the profundity of our own ignorance, because we *know* we have no clue, no inkling, no possible way of understanding any part of what's transpiring. We don't know *the first thing* about what's going on or what to think or how to act or feel.

The room is quieter than when we are taking an important test, as there isn't even the sound of a paper shifting or a pencil moving. This sense of the world on mute goes on and on, and the silence is compounding, and I'm not thinking about President Kennedy at all; instead, I'm trying to remember silences that might be analogous to this one.

The only other experience I have with a period of extended quiet is on Good Friday, when my aunt picks us up early from school and drives all six of us off to St. Nicholas Parish in Encino. We're supposed to have fasted by not eating lunch, which we may or may not have done. Once at St. Nicholas, we have to march in, hands clasped in front of us, to genuflect while crossing ourselves as we enter the pew, which is right in front since my aunt and grandmother tithe, something we're not supposed to know about but do.

Then we're supposed to kneel and remain kneeling for some interminable period of time, during which there isn't even a sermon to semilisten to, to be quietly critical of, as we were when Father Church spoke of plugging in the Holy Ghost *like a vacuum cleaner!* or like any other *common everyday appliance!*

Father Church is who we got when Father Gerhardt left—Father Church is pretentious and speaks in what my mother calls the English Major accent, which means managing to sound round-voweled—she says it *vowel-ed* to rhyme with *hallowed*, as in these *hal-low-ed halls.* The English Major accent makes you sound like some poor kid from the wrong side of the tracks, she says, who's sent to Yale on the Poor Pitiful Me scholarship.

During Good Friday services there is no pomp, no music—all we do is kneel and kneel and supposedly pray, and this takes up some incalculable part of the four-hour service that's supposed to represent the Stations of the Cross.

And it being Good Friday and not Sunday, we are not dressed up, so the little boys—Geo and Thomas—have that playground smell that is dirt and sweat and their stinky Keds, and my aunt and my cousin Lizzie

and I—like all the other women and girls in the Episcopal Church—
must cover our heads. My aunt is an expert milliner—the hats she wears
on Sundays are so stylish and amazing that even I am sometimes awed
by them—but this isn't the day for fancy hats.

Today is all about only the darkness, which is the death of the Son
of God, so Aunt Nan and I are in regular clothes and have lace mantil-
las on our heads. These are the black veils she and her mother buy on
Olivera Street in Old Town L.A.—these drape over our heads and on
either side of our faces, like auxiliary hair.

Lizzie's head is covered, too, but since she isn't yet confirmed, hers
is this round lacy doily thing that's stuck to her hair with a bobby
pin and looks like it came off the back of some old lady's overstuffed
armchair.

The air in the church is thick with incense and the cross is covered
with a black drape and some of us may have actually fasted, as we were
supposed to, so our stomachs are growling audibly. We smirk when
we hear them roil and grumble. Lizzie is sitting on the other side of
my aunt at the end of the pew and is still a little girl and good, so she
doesn't act up.

Though Lizzie doesn't yet misbehave, Graham, Jordy, Geo, Thomas,
and I can all hardly contain ourselves once we begin to notice, while
kneeling, how our bellies seem to almost be *speaking to one another!*
One rumbles, another gurgles back an answer, and the next time someone's belly makes a noise, someone—and this is probably Thomas—
starts trembling with laughter, and Jordy, who's sitting between my
aunt and me, turns to me and announces in a church whisper, *Bowel
sounds excellent,* which is the kind of pseudomedical phrase he's heard
on some TV show like *Ben Casey* or *Dr. Kildare.*

And his saying anything about *bowel sounds* would have been
bad enough, but he's pronounced it in Fred Harvey Army Bus, so it

sounds like this: *Boooowel sooooooonds exsuuuulooont, Dooooktur Koooolduuuuur.*

Froood Hoooovey Armooooy Booooos is a private language—I think Thomas may have been the one who actually invented it spontaneously on a car ride home from our grandmother's house at the beach. Jordy and Geo and Thomas were all lying in the way back of the station wagon like sunburned and sandy cordwood, pinching and shoving, as usual, when Thomas piped up to say, Loooooook, looooooook! It's a Frooooood Hoooooovey Armooooooy Boooooos. It sounds a little bit like Gaelic.

A Fred Harvey Army Bus, whatever that is. I've never been clear on this, except that it's something somehow old-fashioned, maybe something from Before.

Whatever it is, Thomas saw one on the freeway.

We speak like this mostly in the car, and mostly because my uncle really desperately hates it and will try to reach around to swat anyone who makes any kind of Froood Hoooovey–ish sound like that. He also hates for boys to sing in falsetto—Oh, Denise, sooo-be-dooo-o, sooooo in love with yooooooou, Denise, blah-blee-bloooo.

But it's the thought of the term *bowel sounds* that has *completely* torn us down in church, and now we've all started laughing so hard we're completely gone, faces buried in our hands, our whole bodies shaking, side muscles cramping, hiding our wet faces, as the rest of the congregation, all seated behind us, must be wondering just what it is about the Death by Crucifixion of Our Lord Jesus Christ that makes Nan Snowden's little monsters, who occupy the most prominent pew, laugh themselves sick in church.

∞

It's later in third period that the principal comes on the PA to tell us that the president has died at Parkland Hospital, and that we are now on an abbreviated schedule. The B-9s through B-12s are to go immediately to lunch, and the A-9s through A-12s will follow. After lunch, we're all to return to homeroom in order to be dismissed.

And I see that Señor Gallegos is doing what no one in my family ever does—aside from Grandmother Delia, who cries when she's drunk—which is weeping openly.

So we gather up our books and go to our lockers to get our lunches, to go to the cafeteria or back to homeroom, and there's this festive air of release and excitement. We're being *dismissed*, turned loose, which has never happened before. We're getting out of school and our parents don't know this, so there's a huge surge of energy that has nothing to do with what's going on in Dallas and everything to do with where it is in the San Fernando Valley we can go to get in some kind of trouble.

Drugs haven't happened yet, but you can feel them on the edge of things, waiting like the crisp paper wrapping on a noisy present.

And I'm heading across the quad to my locker when Greg Cox, who's a friend of my cousin Graham's, calls out to me: Hey, Cuz! We're all going to Big Bob's on Reseda. Need a lift?

Some of Graham's friends call me Cuz because he does, and this is when I realize that they're lofty juniors and a grade ahead of me, and because the lunch recesses haven't happened, the news of my spastic face hasn't traveled far enough up the beach to get to them, so I've been miraculously saved.

I'm still Cuz to them, still related to my Snowden cousins, and though word will eventually filter upward, the enormity of what's happened to our president has actually altered not only *now* and the future, but also the time that came before. My problem has been altered now, diminished by this event, which is *historic*, and it's just this pretty tiny thing that happened in the life of me and that time is already rendering insignificant.

෮෮෮

The TV is suddenly on in every house I walk by, on in our house in the daytime, which has never happened before, and my aunt is almost entirely quiet, which is her no-nonsense way of dealing with uncertainty. People are saying maybe it's the commies who did it, since Lee Harvey Oswald is married to a Russian girl, though the Poors, who live directly behind us and are John Birchers, say this theory doesn't make sense, since JFK was himself a pinko.

President Kennedy was not a *pinko*, my aunt says. He was a liberal Democrat and Janet Poor is an idiot, and on that, she adds, *you may quote me.*

And strangely, we're allowed to hang out in the house, drinking lemonade, eating Fritos and stale Girl Scout cookies from a cupboard in the garage that my aunt keeps locked, and we're watching TV during the daytime because this keeps us home and out of the way of whatever might be going on out there, and Aunt Nan is watching TV herself, which she never does, and in any case we're not paying that much attention.

My aunt's distracted because my uncle's driven off to a Brown Bag lunch with his investment group, because they need to talk about what the death of the president is doing to the stock market. My aunt doesn't agree with his behaving like this.

And it's because she doesn't agree with his doing this, or maybe doesn't know for sure that he's coming home to eat with us, that she fixes a kid dinner that night, which is spaghetti and meatballs, the sauce made with an envelope of Lawry's, and a salad and french bread. All us kids love such a dinner, but my uncle can't really stand it, so we never eat this kind of thing unless he's traveling or out with Visiting Firemen.

My uncle doesn't like what will later come to be known as *pasta* but is then still known as *noodles* or *macaroni*. He doesn't like anything with all the basic food groups confused or mixed together, anything resembling a *casserole*, which is dreary, he says, and is what poor people bring to funerals.

It's Geo's turn to say grace. We say the same thing every night, which is Bless O Father These Gifts to Our Use and Us to Thy Service, For Christ's Sake, Amen, which for us is breathed in one or two exhalations: *Blessofatherthsgiftsouruse, usthyservisChristsakeamen.*

And dinner is tense because of the spaghetti and meatballs, which my uncle, who has come home to eat afer all, may believe is a form of vengeful cooking, so he's visibly miffed. Then he says he got a bunch of tickets to the Rams game this Sunday from someone in his Brown Bag group who's not using them, and he asks which of us are going.

Cuz? he asks, starting with me, as he's started down the right-handed side of the dining table, as the three right-handed ones lie to the right of him. I'm startled because he's never called me Cuz before.

Sure, I say, because it's my nature—if I'm not sulking—to want to go everywhere and do everything, and I've never been to a pro football game before and it'd probably be especially fun with my uncle, who's generous and lenient and might let us play KFWB really loudly in the car, and who can usually be counted on to buy us the exact kind of crap my aunt will not allow us to touch—for instance, Pepsi-Cola, which, very famously, is only sugar, which ruins your teeth.

Then I notice that no one else has chimed in, and I see my aunt glaring at him, her nostrils flaring. Edward, she asks, using his full name, which she never does, do you imagine a *Rams game* is actually *appropriate* under the circumstances?

He crosses his eyes, face gone slack and goofy, which is for the benefit of us kids. It's like he's been cartoon pole-axed and his head's about to do a 360 on his neck, and he'll now lose consciousness like Elmer Fudd when Bugs Bunny slams him on the head with some huge wooden mallet, and the thought balloons will all be bubbling up like fireworks full of the *X*'s and exclamation marks of many blanked-out curse words, and the soundtrack will be this lullaby played in twittering birdsong.

Then Uncle Ned immediately snaps out of it.

Oh, I never know any longer, he says—and his voice is thick with sarcasm—what is and is not appropriate, Nan, so why don't I leave all that *to you*? And he pats the meatball on his plate with the back of the tines of his fork, and we notice that his food is entirely untouched.

And we're all just stricken, shocked, since the two of them never fight and this sounds like a fight to us. The world's in chaos! My aunt and uncle are fighting! The president has been shot!

Geo, he tells my brother, in order to change the subject, you don't launch your whole piece of bread toward your mouth like it's a plane coming in for a landing. You break it on your plate, like this, and your plate is also where you butter it. My uncle demonstrates his classy manners for Geo, as if to show my aunt he can use manners if he *decides to*.

All right? my uncle goes back to asking, because Uncle Ned isn't a person to be either sidetracked or dissuaded and isn't one to waste good tickets to a Rams game when the seats are on the fifty-yard line.

Okay? he says. Who else is going?

But everyone is quiet, so he polls my brother and cousins one by one—all the right-handed side of the table, then up the left-handed side—and everyone, astonishingly, begs off, even Graham, who's a sports fan and whom I'd completely counted on to go, even Jordy. I would never have said I'd go if I hadn't assumed that at least my two older cousins would be going, and now going with my uncle is like being in trouble *because* of him.

Even Geo and Thomas just hang their heads, though they'd ordinarily be the first to jump at any kind of fun, so in the end the tally says it's only me and my uncle, and I'm only now realizing the degree to which I've been so totally *had*.

Who is and isn't going to the Rams game the Sunday after the assassination of John Fitzgerald Kennedy becomes this hinge in the narrative, the contingent event, that place where the trail divides and some folks take the high road and others take the cutoff toward the Humboldt Sink on their way to Donner Pass.

It's like a referendum on their marriage, though this, technically and on paper, is still a strong and stable marriage that will endure, at least technically, until their last child—and this is Lizzie, who's now only eight or nine—leaves for college.

But it's as if we've discovered that this solid ground we're used to is a slip-strike fault, and right now something shifts and gives.

Which reminds me of the months that lay between the death of my grandfather and my own father's death, as it was during that period of time that I kept having the dream that gripped me with fear because it seemed to foretell the future.

I dreamed my parents were fighting, the road in front of our house was cracking open, and that my father was on the far side of the crack and our mother was on the same side as we were, with our house, and that as the crack widened, I had to choose whether to jump or not.

Because no one ever argued in our family. Because voices were not raised. This was not *done*.

My parents never fought, aside from the one time Welton Becket was trying to move my father to Dallas or Houston, Texas, to build these new cities, but these places were *nowhere*, as far as my mother was concerned. And Texas would have been a promotion for my father, in that he'd have been heading up a project group, but she wouldn't even entertain the thought or go on the weeklong trip Becket proposed to simply take a look it.

My mother had her principles and this was one of them: Texas was a shithole dump full of the most objectionable kinds of people.

He wanted her to at least go on this trip with him, but she said she'd never before set foot in Texas and wanted to keep this perfect record.

Our parents fought and their voices were raised, and this was such an unusual event that they didn't notice Geo and me sitting right there where we were hiding under the kitchen table.

They fought and he did not win and they stayed in California, where each together and separately came to grief and my father *cracked up*, and because he was not speaking to his father, it was Uncle Ned who had to fly to Illinois to bring my grandfather's body home on the train for burial, our grandfather having gone to Illinois to visit certain cousins.

And it was during this time—after my grandfather died but in advance of the day, which was the twenty-sixth of February, when my father took his life—that I kept having the earthquake dream in which the street split open and he'd be on the far side but reaching back to us, as if we could either save him or jump across and be with him. I loved my father, who, while sad, was also tall and witty and elegant, and was also a man, while my mother—and this was one of my family's deepest secrets—was already crazy before he died, so his death wasn't really what caused it, and I didn't want to be stuck with her, her insanity, so always, always, at the very last moment in the dream, I leapt.

Not one of my cousins is going to the Rams game except me, as I've been totally tricked into this magnificent act of disloyalty to my aunt, who's miffed at me, but I can't do anything about it without being disloyal to my uncle, who's lately become one of my more ardent fans.

We have five more tickets to give away, but most kids' parents won't allow them to go, given that the country's in this terrible state and Monday's a national day of mourning, so we get it off from school.

When we get home from church that Sunday, my uncle has the TV on in the family room, and as we're setting the table for breakfast, we all see the telecast that shows that as they're moving Lee Harvey Oswald from one place in the jail to another, or maybe to the courthouse, this nightclub guy comes out of nowhere and shoots him in the stomach, and then Lee Harvey Oswald is also taken to Parkland Hospital, where he also dies, and this is when my aunt goes over and turns the TV off, saying, *That* will be enough of *that*.

So I spend a long time calling around to nearly everyone I know, and finally find that Reggie and Steve are allowed to go to the game, maybe because they're football players, or more likely because they've lied to get out of the house, and my friend Jane Brown can go, because her parents are divorced and her mother works all the time as an accountant at Kmart, so the rules of her house are written mainly by her two older brothers, who are twins and jocks. And my friend Suzie Witucki can go because her parents, who manage an apartment building, are alcoholics, so she gets to do whatever she wants.

My uncle likes Suzie and sings some college football fight song using what he pretends is her last name, but he says it as *Go, Windsock-i*, which may have something to do with the state of Wisconsin, or maybe not.

So there are the six of us at the Rams game being played in L.A. Memorial Coliseum, which holds a hundred thousand people. The day is beautiful, the sky cold and clear, and the stadium is pretty full, considering that the year before, the Rams had their worst season ever, as Steve and Reggie are pointing out; Jane Brown knows a lot about football, too, which she probably gets from her older brothers, both of whom once played football for our school.

My aunt was furious at breakfast at those who decided to go ahead and play this game even as our slain president was lying in state in the Capitol rotunda.

Too much at stake, my uncle said from behind his paper. He was eating toast and reading the inside of the newspaper, whose headlines were two inches tall and shockingly thick and black with ink. He was doing this though we're actually not allowed to read at the table.

You mean money? my aunt asked. My uncle shook the paper a little to straighten it and didn't answer her.

Before the kickoff, the announcer comes on the loudspeaker to ask us all to stand for "The Star-Spangled Banner" and to request that after it's sung, we all remain standing to observe a moment of silence in memory of our fallen president.

And we do, and it's the silence of so many that becomes profound, the communal hush of all of us being quiet together as the reality sinks in and what seems like the silence of the eons begins to envelop us, and it's into that silence that the Blue Angels fly.

The sound is deafening, like the sky is being torn open. There are five jets in the formation, and it's the Blue Angels' showing up that finally gets my uncle, who is a hard case and thinks he's been inoculated for all time against grief by what he went through in his youth.

But my uncle flew as a navigator in the Navy in the Second World War, and our president fought in the same war and in the same branch of service, so my uncle sees the loss of the president as his loss, too, and he puts his arm around my shoulder and we stand side by side, our faces tipped upward, as the jets—which are F-11s, as he'll tell us later, built not by his company, which is Lockheed, but by McDonnell Douglas—twist and rise as one thing into the perfect sky, a diamond that dips and tilts, and as it comes roaring back over us, a solitary jet veers off.

And in going way faster than the speed of sound, their wings are pushing the shock waves ahead of them, and as these waves build up, they'll actually fold sound back upon itself so the waves are physically compressed. What you hear in a sonic boom is the air breaking loose as all that that pent-up redoubled sound's released.

The air breaks and falls around us. Time breaks too, I've always felt, as the future comes spilling toward at certain times in wave upon bright wave. I understand that we are all subject to these currents and history as we never seemed to be before. Before, back when we thought the American story was the one about all the progress we were making toward our own perfectibility.

Instead, history is like gravity and it applies to us, and Time moves in one direction only, and this applies to us, and History is turning out to be the ghost that stands up like something out of Shakespeare and silently points the way we've come, saying this guilt too applies to us, we are not exempt from it.

The air breaks apart and the sound of that falls around us. Time is shown as a hinge that swings wide at a moment like this, when the door of the future suddenly gapes open, as if you've come to the edge of an ancient sea.

The death of the president is the same as the death of my father, I see, in that it is all one loss, as the Lost Flier shows, and I am different in that I became good at loss so early, which is what makes me like my uncle.

Time changes us. Before, as Americans, we'd thought we were oddly impervious to history and didn't really believe it even *applied* to us. Before, back when the story we thought we were writing had to do with how we were just like God.

2

A POCKET HISTORY OF SEX IN THE TWENTIETH CENTURY

9
Climbing Out a Window

So IT's ALL THESE years later and we're living in Berkeley and everything's the same, just as it is all also completely and utterly different. I
am still the person I always was, which is the girl who'll be calmly going
along, masquerading as responsible, then will simply find myself mildly
watching as I begin to build the anatomically accurate body in my bed,
then climb out my current window.

Building an anatomically accurate body in your bed, then climbing
out a window, is, I've found, very much like what it is to be a novelist.

I am simply overcome, at times, by the need to escape my present
circumstances, to strike out for The Territories, as my forebears did,
which, if truth be told, might turn out to be even the most *unlikely*
place, as long as it's somewhere else, *anywhere*, as long as it's just not
right here. *California* seems lately like almost a state of mind as much as
it does an honest-to-god *locale*, and if you're born here and raised here
and you have virtually no relatives who were not born here and raised
here, you don't even get to *go visit* people from other places, and so have
no experience of Elsewhere. And California is such a long state from end

to end and is so far west that you can drive for literally days without ever arriving anywhere that strikes you as a plausible destination.

So a place like Berkeley or L.A. will feel like it exerts an almost centripetal force on the soul of someone like me, a place where even the light can seem like something that etches the pavement with acid shadows, leaf-shaped, ghostly, tinting the lines and cracks in the concrete with the vegetable stain that speaks forever of brokenness.

And we're living in the big gray-shingled house Jack and I have bought on Virginia Street in the flats two blocks below Shattuck. This house has an old thick-trunked wisteria vine growing over an arbor that crosses the drive, and there's the falling-down building out back he's going to fix up for me as a writing studio. This shed was once used as a garage or carriage house, but it's much too small for my SUV, the seven-seat-belted mommy car I drive and drive and drive, making all these countless carpooling trips that involve hauling my two interesting kids and their interesting friends around to all these expensive, tightly booked, enriching activities.

Because I am perhaps predictably in disguise these days as one of those chardonnay-swilling, Volvo-driving, albeit left-leaning, very *bourgeoisified* Berkeley types—that everyone, including me, hates, though I break from type in that I'm much too much a student of Marx and Veblen and Flaubert to do anything so conspicuous consumption–ish as to actually *drive* a Volvo, and I cannot, of course, *drink*, given the sodden, oh-so-severely alcoholic matrix that's deeply embedded in my twisted helix wherein my genes are copied by the eerie legacy of the two so closely matched pairs of my very closely matching parents. And all this has been actually proven fairly recently in my going abjectly to hell over the recent dissolution of my marriage to the father of my kids, which—given *both* nature *and* nurture, given my shitty childhood, given what is clinically called *early death of a parent,* given all the other tragedies best enumerated as what my mom called all that blah, blah, blah—has very spectacularly failed.

When their dad and I split up, I sublet a house from a wine merchant who had an amazing cellar to which he graciously offered access, so while this man was off traveling in Italy and France, I became more and more deranged by my own grief and disappointment, and would dye my hair bright shades of mahogany or walnut—once, it was the deep purple of aubergine—and smoke cigarettes. And in trying not to weep until I dropped my kids off at Point A or Point B, I'd not particularly surreptitiously chew my way through the childproof caps of the bottles of Valium I kept in the pockets of my jackets. Only after I'd made it through the day and tucked my kids in at night did I get to *finally* sit down at the typewriter with a bottle of really fine pinot grigio. I'd be drinking as I was trying to write another novel, but what I wrote when I was drinking was—as has been said of the lesser work of Hunter Thompson—nothing but coo-coo spit.

⬡

I was in graduate school when I met the man who would become my kids' dad. He was my professor, and he was *exactly* the age my father was when my father died. He was somewhat older than I was, of course, and gloomy and smart and strange, also cynical, also a little devious, which probably read to me as *mystery*, and all this figured so clearly in what was very obviously *in loco parentis*.

I had this conceit going from my childhood that I secretly *knew* what men needed, any man, one like my dad or even a more ordinary man, like my uncle. It was like whatever's the opposite of an Oedipal thing, but I do not mean Electra. It was this generalized contempt that I carried for the older version of what my mother called Our People, in that I knew that in being a girl I could so totally do such a better job of making any man happy than any actual *woman* could, so why didn't women not exactly die, but more just *move over* and get out of my way?

In that my professor in grad school's wife had just dumped him and he had these kids already, whose hems were falling down waifishly out of their homemade seventies-hippie-children skirts. But I knew how to sew, even hemstitch, and I knew how to make both chocolate éclairs and potstickers, so the professor's little family seemed to have such simple needs that I could so easily fill.

And Berkeley then may have been, and may still be, one of the best places in the world to go shopping for new wives and husbands, but it does often happen that it's the wife who dumps this kind of sad-sack guy and you see these men all the time in the produce aisles of Andronico's Park and Rob, with their little handbasket for one and their air of slightly unkempt, befuddled, hapless anxiety. Honestly, it takes about five seconds of shopping among the peaches and nectarines of the Park and Rob to find all kinds of prospects, and many of them have advanced degrees from really excellent universities.

My professor had these waifish daughters, one of whom was *exactly* my age when my own dad died, but it was at the very moment he confided that he was in psychoanalysis—then immediately clarified that this *wasn't* the New Agey kind of crap wherein you call your therapist by his first name and go out with him for coffee, but the old-world, Germanically accented, über-strict-ish variety that is actually the *Freudian analysis* that has you lying on the couch, reading squiggles on the ceiling, as my parents had, this being the therapeutic approach that was so entirely unhelpful, given the monumental troubles of the two of them—that I suddenly knew what my future held. It was when he pronounced the word *psychoanalysis* that I seemed to hear a heavenly choir singing, *Dun*-dah-dun-*dun*, in that *immediately*—and I mean *right that very second*—I was very deeply involved with him.

Within the fortress of this rule-bound and non-New Agey marriage, I bore my own two very interesting children and wrote a book I'm still proud of.

Jack published it. This is how I met him.

I'd written this book, which took a long time to do, and I was now completely torn down and really discouraged that I'd even live to see it published, as I'd become pretty sick with one of these stress-related illnesses that almost invariably afflict women of childbearing age, and mine was the one in which you suddenly become allergic to almost everything in your environment, including, and increasingly, the scent of your professorial husband's shaving cream.

So when Jack called, it happened that I'd been in bed in a darkened bedroom for more than a month with a raging headache, extreme light sensitivity, and a persistent low-grade fever. My husband was home to answer the phone. He told Jack I was sick, that I'd call back later.

They don't phone to reject your book, I said as I got up out of bed, phoned Jack, and began to feel much better almost instantly.

The rheumatologist I was seeing explained it this way: A wired-up lab rat in a closed box will, when repeatedly shocked, quickly die, but if you show this rat an open door or a little cracked-open window, *just the sight* of an exit will act to save its life and you can go ahead and zap it a hundred times.

It was during the editorial process that I started to get to know Jack, and so discovered that he, too, was going through a rough patch. It evolved naturally that I became one of his little cadre of sympathetic listeners, most of whom were women, all of whom were married or otherwise unavailable, so there was no blur in the distinctions. He'd call and ask one of us out to lunch, or maybe for a drink or dessert at Chez Panisse after his stop-smoking class.

That was when Jack was still sitting up in his beautiful house in the Berkeley Hills, huddled in a wooden folding chair in the kitchen by the koi tank, listening to the Giants' game on the radio and smoking cigarettes, while he waited for his wife to come home. Late spring through summer and fall, it was the Giants; then he changed and listened to Cal football. And if you talked to Jack on his home phone during that period—which I didn't, but so said Ross Feld, our mutual friend—you'd quickly realize Jack *really needed* to hang up, so worried was he that she'd phone that exact minute to say she'd decided to come home, but if she got a busy signal or the machine picked up, she'd probably change her mind.

Everyone who knew them knew she wasn't coming back, knew all Jack's endeavors were useless—his putting in a new and glamorous downstairs bathroom that opened onto a deck with a hot tub and a view through the treetops of the lights of San Francisco; his redoing the kitchen with the eight-foot koi tank, the Sub-Zero fridge, Wolf range, sinks, and cabinets all put together left-handedly in deference to this left-handed wife. No one said anything; everyone was being patiently mindful and respectful of his household activities, which had everything to do with the hopelessness of denial that rigs the mind with these strings of tiny icy lights like it's Christmas way off there in the coldest part of the darkest and most distant desert.

It already was the brand-new day, the bright harsh glare of the new reality, but Jack wasn't ready to go out into it.

So he and I'd have lunch and I could see his situation clearly, just as he could see what I couldn't see, which was the hopelessness of mine. I'd be bragging and lying, as usual, about my first having successfully raised myself, *despite all odds and with almost no assistance!* then having worked my way through college as an emancipated minor, since I'd been thrown out of my more extended family for the usual infractions, mostly having to do with my surliness and lack of gratitude.

And I'd be bragging and lying about how I'd made this fairly wonderful marriage to this really decent man with several advanced degrees from a truly prestigious university, when my physical person was actually increasingly allergic to him, which I made a point of never mentioning to anyone, including myself—this *good man* who was so good, in fact, he somewhat surprisingly imported his widowed mother from Queens to live with us, which was—*no! no! really, perfectly fine with me! No, really! I really liked* my mother-in-law, who was courteous and easy.

She actually was sweet natured and in her early seventies and in remarkably good health, discounting the fact that she was in the midstage of Alzheimer's disease. But I was becoming an expert on all the types and various forms of dementia, which are actually clinically interesting.

Exactly what the thinking was that had resulted in the importation of the Alzheimer's mother-in-law wasn't something I could recall, in that one aspect of my stress-related illness was this brain fog in which my own cognitive function was impaired and I had, by then, almost entirely lost all my problem-solving capabilities. No kidding, it manifested itself as an almost complete inability to properly sequence episodic time.

I'd need to drop one kid here, the other one way over there, while *concurrently* I'd need to be driving the Alzheimer's mother-in-law to her own daycare, which was in exactly the opposite direction. It was that these events were set up to take place *simultaneously* that always just vexed and stymied me.

I'd think about this for a moment and my brain would seize up, just as the hard drive on a computer freezes, and I'd stare mindlessly into the middle distance, thinking, *I'll think about this again in a little minute.*

I believe the decision making may have gone something like this: The Alzheimer's mother-in-law was living alone in her house, with nothing to eat but the ten-pound block of Poverty Program cheese in the fridge, which wasn't an object she or anyone else could decipher. Since she was increasingly childlike and I was already home with our two kids, who were also childlike since they were actually *children*, another kid-type person could be added to the mix, which I'd then handle with my usual jaunty calm.

Because I was actually unusually generous and good natured about everybody's frailties, as I was already completely used to fairly flawed, unusual, cracked, and spackled families. I was also good at finding the heartwarming story in any scene of domestic chaos, which was just such great material. And I could already riff hilariously on how my mother-in-law—who now lacked any kind of adequate ego—had taken to shadowing me around the house, humming mindlessly, or else it might have been little snatches of what can only be called *ditties*. She'd get one little ditty in her head—it might be the first couple of bars of *I'm a little teapot, short and stout*—where it simply stayed and stayed, playing on tape loop, and I'd be opening a couple of cans, doing two different tasks and trying to solve the puzzle of simultaneity, and she'd be humming and I'd be suddenly *overwhelmed* with the need to give our Cavalier King Charles spaniel the Progresso and feed my mother-in-law the dog food.

But no, really! she was only trying to be helpful! as she followed me from room to room, humming as I put a chicken into the oven, but when I would come back a while later to check on it, I would find that the little teapot had snuck in and turned the oven off because she still managed to think she needed to remember this adage, which was *Safety first!*

Safety first! she'd say, wagging a crooked finger at me as if I'd been trying to pull a fast one.

∞

So Jack began taking me to lunch. Our lunches would be editorial in nature, and at one of these he told me I had handed in the *penultimate* draft of my manuscript, and I thought, *Great. Just my luck to have an* editor *who doesn't know what the word* penultimate *means.*

But I in fact was rewriting the book and did eventually rewrite it a time and a half, then another time after it was already in galleys, because the book in fact was all sprawling and stuttery and was always way too long and was never very good, but then it miraculously was and it was going off into the world, so we'd finished our editorial work but he and I'd still be strolling up Solano Avenue to this or that little restaurant as summer turned to fall turned to winter, and because I was still suffering from the lingering symptoms of the stress-related illness, including a sun allergy, I wore what can be described only as these fairly elaborate costumes whose style was somehow hip-hop crossed with Claude Monet.

I wore huge dark sunglasses and wide hats and long sleeves and full billowing dresses that fell to my ankles in black and gray. Because I was wearing zinc oxide on my face and arms in order to be able to swim, my professor husband had started to refer to me jocularly as Mrs. Vincent van Gogh, the joke being that my last name is Dutch, but also that I was (secretly) crazy. My being (secretly) crazy was one, in fact, of the rock-solid tenets of our marriage.

It went like this: I was crazy and artistic, so my judgment was skewed, just like some wacko Dutch painter who saw the world from this canted and weird perspective that had all the furniture pushed up into the corner of a yellow room. He was Theo to my Vincent and I'd be lost without him and I saw things wrong—my family was *crazy*, while my husband's was only *organically demented.*

And it was true that I also had recently developed an allergy to the thick look of the furniture in our house, which had been already completely furnished on the day the Mayflower truck arrived from Queens and unloaded all of my mother-in-law's furniture into the rooms of our house, so there were now rugs upon rugs upon rugs and tables shoved right up next to these other *really important tables*, if I cared about such things as *really important tables*, which I absolutely did not, and now every room was so clotted with furniture that the place looked like an antiques shop. And then there was also the mundane and everyday clutter of all the physical playthings children need, which were usually strewn in the first ten to fourteen inches of the understory of this forest for the trees, a mix of metaphors that was actually bewildering, since I have figure/ground problems on the best of days, and the kid stuff was often made of that bright plastic in clownlike primary colors, which gave the whole thing a really jumbled look that reminded me of my own mom's housekeeping, or complete lack thereof, and made me feel completely psychotic.

Because of my sun allergy, I'd been investing in actual hats, including one that had a name, which was Springtime, and was made by a genius milliner named Victoria di Nardo who had a shop in lower Manhattan. I bought this hat one day when I was actually dead drunk and it wasn't even noon by my body clock; I'd been out with the PR person for my book. She'd taken me to Victoria di Nardo's shop after we'd had lunch, at which we'd each had who knows how many glasses of champagne to celebrate my brilliant performance on a television show that had taped that morning at the crack of dawn. I'd flown in on the red-eye from Oakland the night before and they'd lost my luggage and there'd been no stores open that early in the morning and the show was scheduled to tape first thing, far off in this really desolate studio in Harlem, the same one they used to shoot Lucy and Desi. The PR woman had come to the hotel to get me dressed while the Lincoln Town Car the production people'd sent was already idling downstairs, and she'd had to knock on the doors of all of these neighbors of hers in her apartment building to borrow all kinds of different potential articles of wardrobe, since she and I had never before met and she had no idea what I might or might not want to wear, let alone what would even fit.

My book was a success, though I'd managed to give it the ballast it needed to make it mine, this being the way I needed to always fuck up in order to keep on being my own parents' child, so the first word of the first book I ever published had as the first word in its title the code word *Failure*. And in the world of publishing, they shorten titles to their first word or so, so while the whole title was *Failure to Zigzag*, I did hear people refer to my book as *Failure*, though I secretly called it *Zigzag*.

The success of *Failure* was an entire shock to my system, and I was okay to good on the TV show, and so went out with the PR person and got completely and utterly swacked and it wasn't even nine thirty in the morning Pacific Standard Time, which was where my body was. And it was only later, when I was completely drunk and shopping and was spending, oh, I don't know, *four hundred dollars* on this thing that wasn't so much a hat as it was Someone's Miraculous Creation Belonging in a Museum Somewhere, that I noticed—with horror—in the hat shop's mirror that not only was I wearing hand-me-downs from people I'd never met, but my face was still entirely made up in the exaggerated lips and eyes and cheeks that they put on you for TV, a look so awful I literally screamed.

ōōō

So back home, I'd still be going out to lunch with Jack though my book was launched, and I'd be hidden behind dark glasses and this $400 hat of mine, which had a wide brim and a fringe of raffia dreads that were almost exactly like a curtain, so while I could see him, he couldn't exactly see me. It was as if I were watching him from another room, as I heard him half rationalizing, patiently justifying, his wife's fairly wretched behavior, and he was so patiently *understanding* of her, which is—as I happen to know—how we all cloak ourselves from the terrible need to tower over our loved ones and rain obscenities down on them.

But Jack had been raised Baptist and was now a practicing Buddhist, so he didn't shout obscenities at women because he didn't shout obscenities at anyone. He really rarely used profanity, and I, too, was probably more carefully spoken than I really am, not saying, for instance, *Oh, for fuck's sake!* at the slightest provocation, because I'd fallen in love with him and wanted him to think I was a person of some kind of, you know, *quality*.

And my love for him was simply overwhelming. I'd never experienced anything like it—I was in love with the resonance of his voice and the beauty of his hands and the tawny color of his skin and the shape of his head and the almost Asian-looking slant of his eyes and the look of his muscular arms. His stories were always miraculously detailed, their endings always both deft and surprising. It was his shy and stately demeanor, and that he was an *enthusiast*. He was hopeful and enthusiastic about almost everything, yet managed to ardently despise his mother because this was realistic, in that she was basically a despicable person. This made no sense according to Sigmund H. Freud, but then, maybe Jack would be living proof of the entire disputation of Freud's lockstep, reductive, fatalistic theories, which had anyway never interested me enough to actually read them, and which I naturally resisted, in that these theories essentially doomed me.

Jack was courteous to his mom: he just didn't feel compelled to *like* her. She was manipulative, he said, and she was cruel. I take these two things as proof of evil in the world, he told me once: my mother and the Republican Party.

But he believed the best about almost everyone else and still thought the errant wife was probably, one day, coming back to him. He wasn't cynical. He had no idea at all of his effect on women. And despite his mother, or maybe even because of her, he actually *liked* women and had as many women friends as he did men. He seemed to listen to everyone with an air of respectful attentiveness, as if this person might have something interesting to say and he, Jack, was maybe going to learn something.

And there was no doubt that it was because I was already so sickeningly married and he was completely unattainable that made it easy for me to love him. It helped, too, that he did nothing to act seductive, in that acting seductive is so often fake.

In those days he'd walk me back to my SUV and open the door, and in his mannerly way that was in no way reserved for me, he'd close the door, then lean in through the open window to kiss me on the lips—but then, he kissed everyone on the lips, I'd noticed. I'd seen him kiss his own grown sons on the lips.

He'd kiss me, then say in parting, So, call me next week and we'll have lunch? and I'd say okay, but I'd be thinking, *But we just* had *lunch*. I didn't think this was *exactly* how the writer/editor relationship was supposed to go, but what did I know, since I'd never before been in one?

So we'd have lunch, then another lunch, and when I was back out on the road again a little while later, promoting my book—this may have been the paperback—it happened that, by sheer coincidence, Jack and I were going to be in New York over the same few days. It was purely lucky in that this happened through neither his guile nor mine.

Neither of us had any control over any of these events: that someone else had arranged that I'd be staying at the Westbury on the Upper

East Side, this being paid for by some media entity that can afford this sort of travel—and it was here, I'd discover, that a bowl of berries with cream and a pot of room-service coffee cost $28, *and this was in the 1990s!*—and Jack was going to be staying at the Algonquin, which was where he always stayed, where he had a sales conference.

As he walked me to the car, he asked me to call him when I got to New York, so that we could go out for coffee or maybe go to a museum together. Call me, he said, looking at me over the tops of his sunglasses, and maybe we can get into a little trouble.

10
The Least Little Push of Joy

It is my profound belief that there is something wrong with me and that it's this wrongness that keeps me loyal to my parents.

I believe in failure. This means *failure* isn't anything I can really part with. My parents were just *so good* at being *such spectacular fuckups*— better than almost anyone. And I'm *proud* of this about them, in that these are *my people*, my own mother and my own father, those I was *born to*, and I have no real wish to ever let them go.

So *failure* profoundly appeals to me, as it feels both true and actual, and I believe in failure in the way I don't basically believe the Success Propaganda that people put out in their Christmas letters, which always seem to stink of the ink of faint Republicanism, and even if this stuff is verifiably, fact-checkably true, it still just doesn't much interest me.

Failure just seems like the more intimate and important news: that you're born, that then you die, and that life between usually stretches as one long grim trudge westward into the hinterlands, and that, sure, there are these bright moments of almost unaccountable joy, but most-ly? mostly? it just is not that. Mostly, it's this story of restlessness and loss and dislocation, but it's also our very strangeness as a lost and dislocated species that accounts for our being funny, and being funny is what elevates us from the basic lies of the Success Propaganda, all that's humdrum and blah, blah, blah. It's being funny that's liberating, that actually saves us.

So it's that we are almost always just *so incredibly lost* that serves as my compass, my ballast, whatever dark, molecularly dense material that's placed in the hold of my soul that gives me stability in heavy seas, and this is why failure is so *valuable* to me and why I keep it stuffed in the most secret pocket of my jacket like a little thingy of Kryptonite.

This wrongness I come by genetically, in that it derives from why people like mine even ended up in the West, where the sun's blaze has suddenly turned against me and my skin has become bizarrely allergic.

The name of this condition is photosensitivity, which is a heightened response to ultraviolet radiation, but what I really think is that I've been oversaturated by the sunniness of the place and its relentless optimism, that my skin—and I have always somehow reasoned with either my belly or my skin—has now just basically *had it*.

I've always done an adequate job of masquerading as an ordinary person, having learned this by living with my aunt and uncle. I've learned to comport myself and think of this as *passing*. I have somehow even tricked this man I love into loving me, and this man isn't even someone flawed and broken and wrecked, like the usual guys who'd come around, all hangdog and slobbery, but someone I actually adore, about whom I was and am still ardent.

What's wrong with me is that I have so many conflicting things going on, and *all at once*, that I feel crowded, also lonely, also buffered and walled off and numb. This pertains to something I've read somewhere: that the dead surround the living, that our work in being alive is to serve as the beating heart of them, that the living and the dead are all